Reincarnation:
The Karmic Cycle

T H E Mananam S E R I E S

(Mananam–Sanskrit for "Reflection upon the Truth")

(continued on inside back page)

THE *Mananam* SERIES

*R*eincarnation: The Karmic Cycle

CHINMAYA PUBLICATIONS
CHINMAYA MISSION WEST PUBLICATIONS DIVISION

**Chinmaya Publications**
Chinmaya Mission West Publications
Main Office
P.O. Box 129
Piercy, CA 95587, USA

Chinmaya Publications
Chinmaya Mission West Publications
Distribution Office
560 Bridgetowne Pike
Langhorne, PA 19053
Phone: (215) 396-0390   Fax: (215) 396-9710
Toll Free: 1-888-CMW-READ (1-888-269-7323)
Internet: www.chinmayapublications.org

Central Chinmaya Mission Trust
Sandeepany Sadhanalaya
Saki Vihar Road
Mumbai, India 400 072

Credits:

Series Editors: Margaret Leuverink, Rashmi Mehrotra
Associate Editor: Neena Dev
Editorial Assistants: Pat Loganathan, Seemantini Nadkarni, & Vinni Soni
Text Layout: Arun Mehrotra
Graphics: Cranberry Blewe
Printed by: Central Plains Book Manufacturing

Library of Congress Catalog Card Number 00-106826
ISBN 1-880687-22-4

Contents

Preface

The word "reincarnation" evokes in most of us mysterious images of past lives. Some of those images can be quite romantic, but to properly understand the theory of reincarnation we need to dismiss the tendency to fantasize about the past and broaden our vision. We need to look closely at the Law of Karma or the Law of Cause and Effect, as Karma and Reincarnation are inseparable. The word karma is used frequently today, but few of us know the depth and breadth of its meaning. As we study the Law of Karma we are reminded of the extraordinary importance of our every thought, word, and deed. We learn that everything we think or do has an effect, not only on a gross physical level, but also on a subtle mental level. Just because we cannot always see the physical effects right away does not mean that it is not operating. Simply put, this law gives us the results of all that we have thought or done. Noble thoughts and selfless actions are, therefore, the language of spiritual progress, "We reap as we sow."

The articles in Part One explain the logic behind the Theory of Reincarnation. Part Two examines the Law of Karma. And Part Three illustrates how freedom from the Cycle of Birth and Death may be gained. The authors point out that the concepts of reincarnation and karma are of great help in finding rational and logical explanations of life's happenings so that we may direct all our energy toward the final goal of Self-realization. It helps us to see that our life is not an accident, but is meant for a definite purpose given to us by the supreme Power. The more we align ourselves with that Power the more we become free from the rounds of births and deaths.

As Swami Yatiswarananda wrote, "Under the spell of ignorance man forgets his divine nature. But there comes a time in the life of every person when he or she begins to feel, dimly or vaguely at first, something about his spiritual nature. The soul of man wakes up, as it were, from its eternal slumber and then begins the struggle to realize its real nature. When the seeker realizes his spiritual nature, and his inseparable connection with the supreme Spirit, all karmas fall off and the cycle of birth and death ends."

The Editors

PART ONE

The Cycle of Birth and Death

The subtle bodies are like water globules.
They may become visible or invisible,
but they are never destroyed.

Swami Abhedananda

Reincarnation is not, as is supposed by many hasty thinkers, a pagan doctrine; it has its roots in the very foundation of the spiritual world. It explains the incongruity of life in light of reason. It offers us consolation in the deepest sense. It makes clear that our disadvantages and our sufferings are not imposed upon us by an arbitrary hand, but are the fulfillment of just laws. It also teaches us that our lost opportunities are not taken away from us forever. We are given new chances so that we may learn and evolve, and set our soul free from the bondage of ignorance. And every time we are born into the flesh we bring with us added knowledge and power from our previous life. Nothing of real value is ever lost; nor are our cruel and treacherous acts forgotten until we have atoned from them.

It is not that some one is keeping account of our thoughts and deeds, but we ourselves keep a complete record of even the things we do in the dark and the thoughts that we entertain secretly in our heart. And we reap the sum total of these thoughts and deeds in our every embodiment. We obtain our body, mind, brain, senses, gifts, merits, and demerits all in accordance with what is best for our evolution. As we evolve spiritually we obtain higher and higher opportunities for self-expression. Even our body and senses evolve greater powers of purity, subtlety, and keener perception. For evolution takes place in every department of our life. There is organic evolution, mental evolution, and spiritual evolution.

Swami Paramananda

Reincarnation and Immortality

I

The Belief In Reincarnation

by Christopher Bache

I came to accept reincarnation only after living and thinking for many years within what I now call the "one-timer's perspective." Reincarnation was not part of the southern Catholic world I grew up in, nor was it taken seriously in the academic world where I pursued my professional training. Through eleven years of higher education, I do not remember hearing a single lecture on the subject. I knew that Hinduism and Buddhism taught the doctrine of rebirth, but I had only distant contact with these traditions at the time. All the thinkers I studied — religious and secular — pondered the riddles of existence assuming that life was a one-time only experience. For all their differences, they accepted this common starting point. Only after completing my graduate studies in philosophy of religion did I become convinced that rebirth was a fact of life. When I shifted to seeing life as a repeated experience, a very different world began to open to me. If reincarnation was one of the fundamental rules of life, we were playing a game very different from what I had thought we were playing.

The question of reincarnation is in essence a question of our life expectancy and through that it becomes an inquiry into the basic nature and purpose of human existence. One of the most basic questions we can ask ourselves is — How much time do I get? How much time do I get to be alive, to take in experience, to learn? How much time do I get to make mistakes and to correct my mistakes, to discover what it is I most want from life and to pursue it? Are we beings that live at best a hundred years, or are we beings that live, say, ten thousand years — through many hundred-year cycles? These are critical questions because how we answer them will profoundly influence what we understand ourselves to be and what we take life to be about. We cannot become more than we have time to become, nor can we expect more from life than it has time to give us. Everything hinges on how many years we have to work with.

If we live only one lifecycle on earth, this constricts what we can expect to realize out of life. We are given just enough time to sort out our individual identity from our family's expectations, train ourselves in some trade, find a mate and raise the next generation, accomplish something professionally, and, if all goes well, relax for a few years with our grandchildren before we die. Along the way we may look up occasionally to marvel at the universe in which we live. We may cry in awe of the miracle of birth or the beauty of the Milky Way. We may even spend years contributing to our collective understanding of some aspect of its wonder. But always we know that no matter how hard we try, we do not have the time to truly explore the extraordinary cosmos we find ourselves in or to participate to any significant degree in its grandeur. On the other hand, if we live many lifecycles on earth all this changes. Our roles in the cosmic drama expand in proportion to the time we are on stage. Reincarnation weds our individual evolution to the larger evolution of the universe, and we become more significant participants in everything that is taking place around us. This inevitably will cause us to raise our philosophical estimate of the purpose of human existence.

The Problem of Suffering

How we answer the question of reincarnation determines our answer to many other important questions. Take, for example, the problem of suffering. Each one of us knows that just one phone call, one doctor's visit, or one careless driver can shatter our world. How are we to respond to the seemingly inexplicable tragedies that so easily cut through our lives, severing relationships and shattering our dreams? The inequities surrounding us in life are so great and the injustices so terrible that they challenge any claim that we live in a universe which permits meaning, let alone a universe which supports our deepest yearnings. On the surface of things, life appears cruel and devoid of compassion. We appear to live at the mercy of whimsy and fortune, to have no control over our fate.

The litany of events that can crush our lives is rehearsed on our television screens every evening. Someone drives home still angry with her boss, runs a red light, and hits a car in which a couple is bringing their newborn child home from the hospital. The wife and baby are killed. Someone else's sanity finally snaps, and he goes on a killing rampage at a nearby shopping mall. As we listen to these stories day after day, how can we not come to feel that we are walking a tightrope over an abyss of random chance that constantly threatens to swallow up everything we love in life? If these tragic events are truly without meaning, then there is no order to our lives and no logic to our fate. Without order, life is random, and if random, tragic. We can survive without the reassurance of meaning, but we can never relax. We can never feel safe in any ultimate sense because we know life cannot be trusted. It pays no attention to our deepest needs, nor does it honor our heartfelt efforts. If even one human life is wasted, if even one human being is treated shabbily by life, then the universe is unjust and none of us can trust it.

How we respond to the questions raised by humanity's suffering will differ profoundly, depending upon whether we start with the assumption that we live on earth only once or whether we view this one life as part of a chain of many lives. If we see life as a one-shot affair, we have essentially two options. First, we can accept the premise of randomness and make do as best we can. If we are only complicated physical beings brought into existence through spontaneous mutation, as so many believe today, then of course there is no genuine meaning to our lives or to the events in them other than what we can give them through a heroic act of will, as the existentialists recommended. If the physical universe is the only universe that exists and if we perish with our bodies, then we live in a world guided only by necessity and chance, operating without purpose or project. We simply must make the best of our luck and keep developing technology to reduce our risks.

The second option is the traditional Western religious one that sees us surviving the loss of our bodies and inheriting a compensatory afterlife that balances out life's injustices in eternity. Unfortunately, this approach leaves the reasons for the original injustices unexplained. They are taken as reflecting the will of God, yet ultimately we cannot understand God's reasons for allowing them. Despite centuries of debate, Western theology has never been able to explain satisfactorily how we can reconcile humanity's suffering with the belief that God is all-loving, all-powerful, and all-knowing. Thus the problem of suffering has become part of the mystery of God.[1]

Yet the anguish that has traditionally surrounded the problem of suffering in Western theology and the resulting inscrutability of God have been forced upon us not by revelation but by the questionable assumption that we live on earth only once. When we introduce the alternative hypothesis that we live many lifecycles here and that our experience in any one cycle can only be comprehended within the context of the others, the world suddenly becomes more complex but also more humane. When we begin to look at the rhythms of life through reincarnationist eyes, the chaos that surrounds us changes into a symphony of exquisite complexity and beauty. Themes started in one century are developed in another and closed in yet a third. The consequences of choices made in one life register in others. All is conserved; nothing is wasted.

For several centuries, scientists have been showing us the incredible splendor and magnificence of the physical universe we live in. From the macro level where galaxies are born and die to the micro level where particles show only "tendencies to exist," the universe demonstrates not only an uncanny precision but also an ingenuity and beauty that cannot fail to move us. Nature is a work of art at every level. Wherever we look in the physical universe we see a world pervaded by order and intelligence.[2] Yet when we turn to consider our own lives, this order seems to disappear, or at least this is how it has looked to us since the Age of Enlightenment. Everywhere around us is the lawful progression of cause and effect, yet at the existential level our lives appear to be riddled by chance. Cause and effect may govern our weather, our physiology, even our psyches, but they do not appear to govern our fate. Thus where it counts most to us, we are cut off from the order that saturates the world around us. If this is the way things are, then the beauty of a spectacular sunset is a cruel joke, for ultimately our lives do not participate in that beauty any more than they participate in the order that produced it.

Adopting a Worldview

Yet the proposal that the existential flow of human life shares nothing of the order and majesty that permeate the physical universe is not forced upon us by the evidence but by the assumption that our lives end when our physical bodies fall apart. When we shift to a reincarnationist perspective, we discover the causality we could not see before. The concept of reincarnation is almost always paired with a concept of cause and effect that orchestrates our many lives into a meaningful sequence. The name given this causal principle in ancient India was *karma,* and most who are familiar with the concept today know it by that name. According to the principle of karma, there are no true accidents in life. Even those events that appear to be without cause in fact have causes buried deep in the fabric of history. In revealing the lawful progression of cause and effect operating in our lives, karma embeds them in a larger natural order. While this natural order is not identical with the natural order of the physical universe, it shares with it the quality of lawfulness. Thus the concepts of karma and rebirth restore our sense of connectedness to the universe we live in. Through them our lives participate in the order and intelligence that surround us on earth, and thus in the beauty as well.

Adopting a reincarnationist worldview tends to change not just our abstract philosophical convictions but also how we meet the concrete challenges posed by our day-to-day lives. You can see this most easily by taking a moment to bring to mind any problem or task you might be wrestling with at the present time — perhaps a relationship, something at work, a financial problem, anything that is currently bothering you. Once you have one clearly in mind, consider how your experience of this situation would change if you saw it as something that did not just appear out of nowhere but came from somewhere definite, with specific purpose and potential for you. How could the adoption of such a posture fail to change your experience of whatever it is you are facing?

The shift is like watching a scene from a play in which suddenly a different and incongruous backdrop unrolls behind the actors. Behind Shakespeare, for example, unfurls the deck of the starship *Enterprise.* Your experience of the scene itself would necessarily change. Imagine yourself one of the actors in this play, speaking your lines, watching for your cues, when the backdrop changes. You try to continue the scene with the same delivery as before, but in your peripheral vision you see that the new backdrop is so different from the first that your lines are losing their meaningful placement in a larger context. Your sense of disparity grows until, good actor though you are, you can no longer continue. "What is going on?" you demand indignantly, your performance hopelessly interrupted.

What is going on, indeed? Adopting a reincarnationist worldview can so change our perception of what we are and what we are involved in that it becomes impossible to continue playing the game by the old rules. We want to know what the "new rules" of a reincarnating universe are. How does reincarnation change our strategies for living our present life?

Footnote

[1] Attempts to make Satan carry the responsibility for the world's pain eventually fail because Satan draws his existence and life force from God and can act only with the implicit permission of God. Attempts to make humans responsible for it through Adam's primal sin will also fail for similar reasons. What kind of architect would God be if his carefully planned creation were to fail his first major test? No, ultimately the riddle of suffering must be laid entirely at God's feet.

[2] The intelligence inherent in nature is obvious, it seems to me, regardless of how we explain it — whether we attribute it to an intelligent creator or to the ingenious mechanism of evolution.

II

Reincarnation

by Swami Chinmayananda

The Hindu teachers, being great masters of renunciation and wisdom, developed their intuitive faculty to such an extent that they could give to the world the most rational theory of reincarnation. All great thinkers from East to West have accepted, expressly or tacitly, the logical conclusions about this doctrine. Buddha constantly made references to his previous births. Virgil and Ovid regarded the doctrine as perfectly evident. Josephus observed that the belief in reincarnation was widely accepted among the Jews of his age. Solomon's *Book of Wisdom* says: "To be born in a sound body with sound limbs is the reward of the virtues of the past lives." And who does not remember the famous saying of the learned son of Islam, Jalaluddin Rumi, who declared, "I died out of the stone and became a plant; I died out of a plant and became an animal; I died out of the animal and became a man. Why then should I fear to die? When did I grow less by dying? I shall die out of a man and become an angel!"

In later times these intelligent, philosophical statements were accepted as doctrine by the German philosophers Goethe, Fichte, Schelling, and Lessing. Recent philosophers such as Hume, Spencer, and Max Mueller have also recognized this doctrine as incontrovertible. And among the poets of the West also we find many burnished intellects soaring into the cloudless sky of their imagination. Within their poetic flights they have also intuitively felt the sanction behind this immortal doctrine — Browning, Rossetti, Tennyson, and Wordsworth — to men-tion but a few. But this theory is not a mere dream of the philosophers and poets. The day is not far off when with the fast developing science of psychology, the West will come to rewrite its scriptures under the sheer weight of observed phenomena. An uncompromising intellectual quest to understand life cannot be satisfied if it is thwarted at every step by observed irregularities. We cannot ignore these irregularities as mere "chances."

Mozart is a spectacular example of a child prodigy that cannot be explained easily. This genius wrote sonnets at the age of four, played in public at the age of five, and composed his first opera at the age of seven! Without the reincarnation theory we have to label his life and talent as just an accident and bury this wondrous incident into the category of chance. Instead, to be logical, we must accept the idea of the continuity of the embodied souls.

The Continuity of Life after Death

The following verse from the *Bhagavad Gītā* asserts in unequivocal terms the truth behind the Reincarnation Theory.

> Just as in this body the embodied (Soul) passes through childhood, youth, and old age, so also, he passes into another body; the learned man does not grieve at it. (2:13)

By using this example as a standard of comparison, Lord Krishna is trying to point out that wise men do not worry when they leave one body for the purpose of taking another. We do not bemoan the death of childhood, after which we come to experience youth. We are confident that even though childhood has ended and youth is entered into, there is a continuity of existence for the same entity. Applying this principle of memory, it becomes quite clear that "something" in us is common in all the stages of our growth, so that the same entity remembers the experiences gained by it in the past through the childhood and youthful bodies.

In the same way, at the moment of death, there is no extinction of the individuality, but the embodied ego of the dead body leaves its previous structure. And according to the mental impressions (*vāsanā-s*) gathered during its embodiment, it becomes identified with another physical body, where it can express itself completely and seek its further fulfillment. Just as an individual changes his clothes to suit the occasion, the ego center discards one physical form and takes to another, which will be most suited for it to gain the required type of experiences.

With the next striking example, the *Bhagavad Gītā* explains how and why the egocentric entity in an individual readily leaves its associations with one set of equipment, and attaches itself to another conducive envelopment for living a new set of required experiences:

> Just as a man casts off his worn out clothes and puts on new ones, so also the embodied self casts off its worn out body and enters into another which is new. (2:22)

Changing clothes that have become worn out cannot be painful for us, especially when it is for the purpose of putting on a new set of clothes. Similarly, when the mind and intellect finds that its embodiment in a given form can no longer facilitate its evolutionary pilgrimage, it feels that this particular form is worn out. This worn-out condition of the body is to be decided by its wearer, the ego; and not by age or by the biological condition. Critics rise up against this idea, however, and their main arguments are based upon the observed examples of those who die at the beginning of life. It is true that the individual was young, but from the standpoint of the evolutionary necessity of the particular ego, the body was already useless for it. A wealthy person might feel like changing his house or his car almost every year, and invariably he finds ready purchasers. As far as the rich owner is concerned, the house has become useless for him, while for the purchaser it is as good as new. Similarly, no one can decide whether a given body is worn out or not except its wearer.

SWAMI CHINMAYANANDA

The Separation of the Subtle Body

The following stanza emphasizes the Doctrine of Reincarnation. Evolution and change are all for the mind and intellect and not for the Self. The Self is ever perfect and changeless, and needs no evolution. Therefore, what goes from body to body is being explained in the following stanza from the *Bhagavad Gītā*:

> When the Lord takes up a body and when He leaves it, He takes these and goes (with them), even as the wind takes scents from their seats (the flowers). (15:8)

When the Lord acquires a body, that is, when the Infinite deludes Itself that it is conditioned by the mind and intellect, it becomes the individual personality *jīva*, and this *jīva* takes various bodies for itself from time to time. It incarnates in different environments that are ordered by the burning desires and aspirations most suited for exhausting and fulfilling its demands. When the *jīva* enters a body it carries the mental faculties and impressions with it and retains them at all times. In fact, the subtle body includes all these faculties.

At death the subtle body permanently departs from the gross body which is left inert. The dead body, even though it maintains the shape of the individual, can no longer express itself, as it has no sense faculty, mental capacity, or intellectual ability. These expressions, physical, mental, and intellectual gave the body an individual personality stature, and all these constitute the subtle body. The gross body bereft of its subtle essence is called the dead body.

At the time of death, the subtle body moves on, gathering into itself all faculties. "Even as the wind takes scents from their seats, (the flowers)." A passing breeze is not separate from the atmospheric air that is everywhere, and yet, when the breeze passes over a flower, or some sandal paste or a perfume bottle (seats of fragrance), it carries with it the respective aroma. Similarly, when the subtle body moves out it carries along with it the senses, the mind, and intellect, not in any gross form, but as a mere fragrance of all that it had thought, felt, and lived. And so the mind is nothing but a bundle of *vāsanā-s*. These *vāsanā-s* can exist only in the Infinite Consciousness; and the Light of Awareness illumining the *vāsanā-s* is called the *jīva*, the individual personality.

In this stanza the *jīva* is called the Lord only to convey the idea that the individual personality is the Lord of the body that orders, commands, and regulates all its actions, feelings, and thoughts. An officer, on receiving his transfer orders from the government, packs up his belongings and moves out of his house, and having reached the new seat of appointment, he unpacks and spreads out his furniture for his comfort. In the same way, at the time of departing from the body, the subtle body gathers itself from the gross dwelling place and on reaching the new physical structure, it spreads itself out again to use its faculties through the "new-house-of-experience."

The Mechanics of the Departure

When the subtle body finds that it has no more experiences to gather with a given physical form living in a given set of circumstances, that subtle form throws away the physical form and leaves. This condition, after its divorce from the subtle body, is called the death of the body, with reference to the body. But the ego-center, (though not manifest and functioning through the body), exists in its subtle form. This subtle ego-center set in the subtle body is conveyed to its next field of activity (*loka*) by the energy called *udāna*. *Udāna*, one of the five *Upa-prāṇas*, is that energy that supplies the motive power for the ego center with its subtle body to move out from one physical structure to another at the time of death.

The *Praśnopaniṣad* says:

> The external fire indeed is *udāna*. Therefore he in whom the
> flames have gone out, enters another body with the senses
> absorbed in the mind. (Q.III:9)

At the time of death an individual slowly loses all sense activities and capacities; he no longer sees, hears, smells, tastes, or feels. This is not because these instruments of cognition have become defective, but the power of perception, meaning the *prāṇik* vitality in the sense organs, is withdrawn. When the ego center with the subtle body prepares to leave the physical body, he, [the chief *prāṇa*], gathers all his different assistants before he makes his exit. Just as when a visitor gathers his coat, gloves, hat, and umbrella we know that he will be leaving soon. Here the *Upanishad* explains that the sense organs, meaning the sense capacities, are withdrawn unto itself by the mind before the *udāna* lifts it from the dying body and guides it along to the next field of activity.

The description of the *udāna* as the external fire, apart from this philosophical significance, has a plain and obvious truth. As long as the *udāna* exists in the human form the person is alive, and as long as the person is alive, there is warmth in the body. When the *udāna* leaves, the heat also goes, as a dead body is cold to the touch. Therefore we can say that a dead body is something from which the flame of life, or the fire, has gone out.

After the death of the body, the ego center remains intact in the form of an "idea" until it comes again to fix a relationship with another form. That which helps the "floating ego" choose its next rendezvous is the sum-total of the reaping it has to make with the new form in the new field of things and circumstances. Indeed, there is no philosophical concept so solid in logic and so true in reason as the law of karma. If properly understood, the law of karma puts the privilege and the power to carve out our destiny into our own hands. According to the quality of the actions performed in the past, we shall have a future existence in a form and in a set of circumstances necessary to reap the required quality of reactions in the form of experiences. Our future lives are dependent not only upon the actions committed in the past, but also upon the degree of knowledge of the Reality that we have gained in and through living the reactions from our past actions. Hence this statement in the stanza from the *Kaṭhopaniṣad*.

> Some souls enter the womb to have a body and others become plants, according to their work and according to their knowledge. (II, sec.V-7)

This stanza indicates the inevitable philosophy of rebirth that is the very backbone of the Hindu faith. This ought to be the sane conclusion arrived at by every honest thinker, if he were to think deeply about life. Had it not been for the karma performed in the past, there would not be so many differences among those who are living now. This stanza hints at the sublime truth, that our present existence is not a mere accidental happening. It is a measured link, shaped by ourselves, which makes the chain of life complete, connecting the dead past through the present and to the unborn future. These words indicate not only that there were many incarnations taken by the ego in the past, but also that it will again continue to manifest itself in numberless incarnations in the future. In short, the present life in this form upon the earth is but an incident in the eternal existence of the Self.

III

Through Experience into Understanding

by Brian L. Weiss

[Brian L. Weiss, M.D. made headlines with his ground-breaking research on past life therapy in Many Lives, Many Masters. *The following excerpt is taken from his book* Through Time into Healing.*]*

Often a new patient or workshop attendee confides to me, "Dr. Weiss, I'm very interested in experiencing past life regression, but I'm having some trouble accepting the concept of reincarnation."

If you feel like this, you are not alone. Many of these people need to address this issue before beginning the regression process. Doing this is often a preliminary part of therapy with these patients, and it is a common topic for questions and answers in my workshops and lectures. Before my extraordinary experiences with Catherine [see *Many Lives, Many Masters*], I myself was extremely skeptical about the concept of reincarnation and the healing potential of past life regressions. Even afterwards, it took several more years for me to make the commitment to bring my new beliefs and experiences into the public eye.

Although Catherine's therapy had radically changed my understanding of the nature of life and the nature of healing, I was hesitant to let other people know about these profound experiences because I was afraid that colleagues and friends would consider me "crazy" or "weird."

On the other hand, I had received further confirmation of the effectiveness of past life therapy by successfully treating more patients with this technique. I knew that I had to alleviate my discomfort to resolve this issue. So I went to the medical library to see if other research was available. The left-brained, logical clinician in me liked this solution to the problem, and I hoped that such validation existed. If I had accidentally stumbled onto past life recall, I was certain that other psychiatrists using hypnotic techniques must have had similar experiences. Perhaps one of them had been brave enough to tell the tale.

I was disappointed to find only a few, albeit excellent, research reports. For instance, I found Dr. Ian Stevenson's documentation of cases in which children appeared to remember details of previous lives. Many of these details were later corroborated by investigative research. This was very important because it helped to provide validating proof of the concept of reincarnation. But there was little else to be found, certainly next to nothing about the therapeutic value of past life regression.

I left the library even more frustrated than when I had entered. How could this be possible? My own experience had already allowed me to hypothesize that past life recall could be a useful therapeutic tool for a variety of psychological and physical symptoms.

Why had no one else reported his or her experience? In addition, why was there almost no acknowledgment in the professional literature of past life experiences surfacing during clinical hypnotherapy? It seemed unlikely that these experiences were mine alone. Surely other therapists had had them.

In retrospect, I can see that what I really wanted was someone to have done the work that I would soon do. At that time I could only wonder whether other psychotherapists were as hesitant as I was to come forward. My research of the literature complete, I was torn between the power and reality of my own direct experiences and the fear that my ideas and new beliefs about life after death and contact with master guides might not be personally and professionally "appropriate."

Reincarnation in Western Religions

I decided to consult another discipline. From my college religion course at Columbia University, I recalled how the major traditions of the East, Hinduism and Buddhism, embraced reincarnation as a central tenet, and how in these religions the concept of past lives is accepted as a basic aspect of reality. I had also learned that the *Sufi* tradition of Islam has a very beautiful tradition of reincarnation, rendered in poetry, dance, and song.

I simply could not believe that during the thousands of years of the history of Western religions no one had written about experiences like mine. I could not have been the first one to receive this information. I later discovered that in both Judaism and in Christianity the roots of belief in reincarnation go very deep.

In Judaism, a fundamental belief in reincarnation, or *gilgul,* has existed for thousands of years. This belief had been a basic cornerstone of the Jewish faith until approximately 1800-1850, when the urge to "modernize" and to be accepted by the more scientific Western establishment transformed the Eastern European Jewish communities. However, the belief in reincarnation had been fundamental and mainstream until this time, less than two centuries ago. In the Orthodox and Chasidic communities, belief in reincarnation continues unabated today. The Kabbala, mystical Jewish literature dating back thousands of years, is filled with references to reincarnation. Rabbi Moshe Chaim Luzzatto, one of the most brilliant Jewish scholars of the past several centuries, summed up *gilgul* in his book, *The Way of God,* "A single soul can be reincarnated a number of times in different bodies, and in this manner, it can rectify the damage done in previous incarnations. Similarly, it can also attain perfection that was not attained in its previous incarnations."

When I researched the history of Christianity, I discovered that early references to reincarnation in the New Testament had been deleted in the fourth century by Emperor Constantine when Christianity became the official religion of the Roman Empire. Apparently, the emperor had felt that the concept of reincarnation was threatening to the stability of the empire. Citizens who believed that they would have another chance to live might be less obedient and law abiding than those who believed in a single Judgment Day for all.

In the sixth century, the Second Council of Constantinople underscored Constantine's act by officially declaring reincarnation a heresy. Like Constantine, the Church was afraid that the idea of prior lives would weaken and undermine its growing power by affording followers too much time to seek salvation. They concurred that the whip of Judgment Day was necessary to ensure the proper attitudes and behavior.

During the same Early Christian Era leading up to the Council of Constantinople, other Church fathers like Origen, Clement of Alexandria, and St. Jerome accepted and believed in reincarnation. So did the Gnostics. As late as the twelfth century, the Christian Cathars of Italy and southern France were severely brutalized for their belief in reincarnation.

As I reflected on the new information I had gathered, I realized that aside from their belief in reincarnation, the Cathars, Gnostics, and Kabbalists all had another value in common: that direct personal experience beyond what we see and know with our rational minds or what is taught by a religious structure is a major source of spiritual wisdom. And this direct personal experience powerfully promotes spiritual and personal growth. Unfortunately, since people may be severely punished for unorthodox beliefs, the groups learned to keep them secret. The repression of past life teachings has been political, not spiritual.[1]

And so I began to understand the "whys." I myself was concerned that I might be punished for my beliefs if I made them public. Yet I know that people have the right to have access to the tools of growth and healing, and I have seen from my own clinical experience that past life regression can heal and transform people's lives. I also know that patients become *better,* more useful members of society and their families, with much more to offer.

But even after *Many Lives, Many Masters* was published, I was still waiting for the backlash. I was waiting for doctors to ridicule me, for my reputation to be tarnished and, perhaps, even for my family to suffer. My fears were unfounded. Although I hear there's a stray colleague or two who has been known to mutter about "poor Brian who's only got one foot on the curb," instead of losing friends and colleagues, I gained more. I also began to receive letters — wonderful letters — from psychiatrists and psychologists throughout the country who had experiences like mine but had not dared to make them public.

This was a powerful lesson for me. I had taken the risk of documenting and presenting my experiences to the public and professional world, and my reward was knowledge, validation, and acceptance. In addition, I had learned that understanding does not always begin with reading accounts of studies in libraries. It can also come from exploring one's own experience. Intuition can lead one to intellect. The twain can meet; they can nourish and inspire each other. They had done so for me.

I tell this story because your concerns — the tug of war between your experiential and intellectual knowledge — might, in essence, be similar to mine. Many people have the same experiences and beliefs you do, perhaps many more than you can imagine. And many of these people feel discouraged from communicating their experiences for the same reasons you do. Still others may be expressing them, but in private. It is important to keep an open mind, to trust your experiences. Don't let the dogma and beliefs of others undermine your personal experience and perception of reality.

Footnote

[1] See *Reincarnation: The Phoenix Fire Mystery* by Cranston and Head for an excellent study on the history of the political and social treatment of the concept of reincarnation in the West.

IV

Preexistence
and Reincarnation

by Swami Abhedananda

From ancient times, philosophers and thinkers from all over the world have tried to unravel the great mystery of nature, the mystery of life and death. Some beings are born and then pass away suddenly without having any opportunity to fulfill all their desires, just as if they are forced by some external power to leave this world unexpectedly before they have completed their life's experiences. Why is this? Why do some people live for a short time and others live longer? Is this all accidental? Do the souls come here and pass away without any definite purpose? Or is there a law behind all these appearances? Our minds want answers to these questions because our tendency is to know and thus we must solve this problem of life and death.

Let us turn for a moment toward different classes of thinkers. The materialists and agnostics deny the existence of the soul as an intelligent self-conscious entity, and they explain everything through material forces, which are governed by mechanical laws. Some of them have gone so far as to assert that the appearance and disappearance of human beings on this planet is nothing but the result of the disintegration of material particles, which are caused by the natural process of the evolution of matter. They claim that all beings cease to exist at the time of death, that there is no soul, there is no purpose in life, and everything comes to us accidentally. But this explanation does not satisfy the minds of the seekers after truth; it does not answer their questions. In the innermost soul of our souls, we know that it is not true. We know that matter alone could not have produced intelligence and consciousness. It would be difficult for any scientist to prove that the combination of matter, or material particles, which are governed by mechanical laws, can produce intelligence and consciousness.

On the other hand, it is a scientific truth that motion produces nothing but motion. But the intelligent soul or consciousness is not a motion, it is not a result of motion, but it is something distinct from motion. It is the *knower* of the motion and all activities. Motion produces nothing but motion. It does not produce the *knower* who has all the power of translating the molecular activities of the brain cells into sensations, perceptions, ideas, desires, and thoughts. All these are the living properties of a living soul that functions in the mind. No one has proven that the brain creates the mind or intelligence, but, to the contrary, the great thinkers of the world have understood the secret of truth concerning the relation between the mind and the brain. For instance, Dr. Thomson, in his book *Brain and Personality* explained that the brain is only the instrument, but the personality, the mind, or the intelligent self-conscious entity overshadows the brain. He compared the brain with a violin. A violin cannot produce any music without a musician. Music is not in the violin, but it is in the mind of the musician, and the musician must bring it out by playing upon the strings that touch our souls. The violin alone cannot do it. In the same way, the personality is like a musician who is playing upon the strings of the nerves and the brain cells from outside, as it were, over-shadowing it and producing either harmony or discord. If the personality/musician is not trained, he will create discord instead of bringing out harmony.

If we analyze in this way, we see that our soul, the self-conscious entity and thinker, is not the result of an activity of the brain-cells, but is something distinct and not composed of any material. Yet it has the power to control and govern all the material forces that are under its domain. If we understand that there is some entity, which is our real Self, who possesses all our desires, thoughts, and ideas, then we want to know That which is self-conscious? Where does it exist? How does it produce this physical body?

Cause and Effect

When we study nature, we find that the law of causation is inexorable. The law of cause and effect governs everything in this universe. Every effect must have a cause. If we deny the law of causation, we not only deny the truth of nature, but also destroy the fundamental principle of modern science, which is that something cannot come out of nothing. This theory has been well advanced by the *Sāṁkhya* theory of Kapila. In fact, nonexistence cannot produce existence, nor can existence come out of non-existence. If we exist today we must have had a cause; we have not come out of nothing.

Applying this truth to the phenomena of life and death, we understand that all the appearances of human beings and other beings on this physical plane have definite causes. Having understood thus so far, we want to trace the kind of cause that produces all these activities of an intelligent being. What is the cause that produces all these things? Is that cause outside of ourselves, or it is in us? A clear understanding of the relation of the cause to the effect is absolutely necessary for the proper solution of any problem that we have to face.

Instead of going into all the details by which the ultimate scientific truth has been established, let us take it as being scientific and correct that the cause of a thing is in the thing itself and not outside of it. It is a fact that the cause of a tree is not outside of the tree, but is in the tree itself. In the same way, the cause of human beings is in themselves and not outside them. We do not have to trace the cause to be outside of us. The cause is the unmanifested state of the effect, and the effect is the manifested state of the cause. The entire tree remains in the seed in an invisible state or in a potential form. The environments only give the favorable conditions, they cannot give any of the powers to the seed that are not already there. If we understand this clearly, then we find that the environments do not create, but the creative power is in the seed itself, and that the seed does not manifest in the causal state until it has taken the form of the tree.

Apply this truth to the human being or to its manifestation. If the cause is in ourselves, then what is that cause? That cause must be something that contains all the peculiarities that human beings can manifest in their lifetime. The cause retains all the potentialities of the forces or powers of the mind, the thoughts, the desires, and the intelligence, just as the seed of an oak tree contains all the peculiarities of an oak tree. Those conditions or powers which are latent in the seed of an oak tree cannot be changed by the environments, but they will manifest into an oak tree and not in the chestnut tree. This is a scientific fact.

The Subtle Being

Therefore, the causal state of a human being will manifest in the future and that causal state is invisible, just as we do not see the potential tree in a seed. The seed of a Banyan tree, for instance, is as small as a mustard seed, and if we saw it we would not know what it is. Yet it contains a gigantic Banyan tree which will cover the area of a mile in circumference and will perhaps produce seventy-five or a hundred trunks of one tree. No other seed will produce that. All the peculiarities of a Banyan tree are in that seed.

Similarly, the invisible germ that we may call an amoeba or protoplasm and which will afterwards appear as a human being, contains all the potentialities of that human being in the invisible state. If we deny this, then we run the risk of having to admit that something has come out of nothing. But the scientific truth is that whatever exists in the end, existed also in the beginning. If in the end we find a human being like Abraham Lincoln, Shakespeare, or Plato then the germ, or the seed from which has manufactured that particular manifestation, contained all those powers in an invisible state. You may call it a germ, or you may call it by any other name. Names do not make much difference. Leibnitz called it Monad. Scientists call it the germ of life. Vedanta philosophy calls it the subtle body. The subtle bodies are the invisible germs or nuclei which contain the mind, the intelligence, the reasoning, the power of thinking, willpower, and all the senses; the powers of seeing, hearing, smelling, tasting, and touching. All these powers are present in the germ of life. It also contains the impressions of the previous manifestation, and those impressions are embedded in that substance. That substance is ethereal or electric, that is, the minute particles of matter which are held together by that force, which is called the life force, or the vital energy.

Now this subtle being is the real man. It appears in the form of a human body, which it manufactures and lives in. Just as an oyster or a crab would manufacture a shell as a dwelling house, so this germ of life or the subtle body of the individual whether it is human or animal, takes only the form according to its desires, or according to its tendencies. The human germ of life will manufacture a human body, and if it desires to be of a particular animal form, it manufactures that form. It has no particular form, but it can take any form. This subtle body contains everything. So we do not gain anything from outside. It is already here; it has infinite potentialities and infinite possibilities.

At the time of death, the individual germ of life contracts all its forces and powers, and all these are centralized into a nucleus and that nucleus retains the life, the mind, the powers of the senses, and all the impressions and experiences that the individual has gathered. Then, in due course, when the favorable conditions exist, it manufactures another form. Parents are nothing but the principal channels through which these germs of life, or the subtle bodies find proper conditions of manufacturing human beings by obeying the laws of nature. Parents do not create the soul. In fact, the parents cannot give birth to a child according to their will. Unless the soul comes to them and nourishes the germ, it would be an absolute impossibility.

These subtle bodies are like water globules. As a water globule may remain in the form of water in the ocean, so it may go up and become invisible in a vapory state in a cloud and then come down again in the form of a drop of rain. Then it may remain again in the mud, or it may be frozen into a solid substance when you can handle the form of a solid substance, or you can handle the form of a piece of ice. But it is never destroyed. It may become invisible or visible. These conditions do not change the globule of water. It is there and this globule of water of the subtle body arises in the beginning-less past, in the ocean of the eternal life, and retains the reflection of the supreme Spirit in the form of intelligence. It may appear on this earth, or it may go to another planet. It has the power to travel with the speed of light. It can follow the way of light from one planet to another with vibrations or waves of the atmosphere. It can shoot out instantaneously. It has such a power. And this subtle body may remain on this plane in the human form. Then after death, it might go to heaven or to some other planet, or remain in an invisible state until the proper conditions and suitable environments are found. Then it gravitates according to its desires.

The entire process is governed by a law. And this law is called the law of reincarnation or remanifestation of the subtle form in the gross physical form. This law is inexorable. Whether or not we admit its existence it works just the same. The same forces, which have brought us here this time, will bring us here again. Who can stop it? Our will cannot stop it, but it will end only when we understand this law, outgrow it, and go beyond it. We can deny it in the same way that ignorant fools may say that they do not believe in gravitation and keep denying its existence, but still they are all being held up by the force of gravity. The molecules of our bodies would fly asunder if there were no force of gravity to hold them together. We could not live on the surface of the Earth if the force of gravity did not hold us down. Still we can deny it. But our denial amounts to nothing and simply betrays our own ignorance that we do not understand the law. In the same way, anyone who denies reincarnation betrays his own ignorance because he does not know the law.

The One-Birth Theory

Those who do not believe in reincarnation believe in the one-birth theory, but they are not able to explain all the inequalities and diversities that we find amongst ourselves. They believe that the souls of the individuals have been created out of nothing; for the first time, and that they will continue to exist forever. How is it possible that anything that has a beginning at one end will continue to exist forever at the other? It is impossible. In the first chapter of Genesis, it says that God created man after His own image. In the second chapter we read that he made man out of the dust of the earth and blew the breath of life into his nostrils…. The writers of Genesis accepted those two stories and put them together in the chapters. But the two ideas are radically opposed. Which will you accept?

If God created man after His own image how did He create Him? The second story said that God created him out of the dust of the earth. But it should be remembered that earth is material, insentient matter and so it does not explain how the breath of life came into existence. All these difficulties that arise in our minds after studying these statements cannot be solved in any other way unless we accept the idea that the spirit or intelligence or consciousness was never created, but the body was created or manufactured through the process of evolution. As the breath of life was never created, so the mind and soul were never created, but the soul retains the image of the Lord, or the supreme Spirit.

In other words, as Vedanta explains, the breath of life contains the reflection of the supreme Spirit that is all-intelligence.

We cannot explain anything by the theory of one birth. Or to believe that the soul is created out of nothing, because if God created the soul out of nothing, why such a variety? Some are born to enjoy and to show their genius and wonderful talents. Others are kept to manifest nothing but ignorance and other weaknesses. How can you explain those things? A person may have five children. One might be a murderer, another might be a genius, and another might be an artist.

What accounts for all these inequalities and diversities? If God creates each one separately at the time of the birth of the body, then who is to be held responsible? Not the parents, but God Himself. Why could He not do better? That question must arise in our minds and we must try to find the solution.

Then another question is raised: Why do some children live only for a short time, for a day, or for a few weeks? Why do they pass away without gaining an opportunity to earn anything, or gain experiences in this vast world of phenomena? Who is responsible and what becomes of those children? Well, there might be a theory that they would go to heaven and enjoy eternal life. Those who believe in that story better pray for the death of their children before they commit any harm. I would do that if I had little children and believed in such a thing. Why should they go through all these miseries and troubles? If we could go straight to heaven by dying in childhood, we would rather die than live.

So this theory does not explain anything but makes life appear absurd and irrational. Then if we admit the theory of predestination and grace that also does not help us very much. If we are predestined and pre-ordained to do these things, and if a murderer is pre-ordained to murder somebody and before he had any will, it was all arranged by the Creator, then why should we hang the murderer? We should hang the Creator, because He is responsible. Therefore we cannot find any solution through this theory.

Heredity

Then there is another theory of heredity. Does heredity explain all these inequalities and diversities? No, it cannot. How can heredity explain the cases of prodigies and geniuses?... Take the case of Goethe, the great German poet. He was an octogenarian poet and philosopher. When he was ten, he was a master of Greek and sixteen other languages. The theory of heredity cannot explain these cases of prodigies and geniuses, but the reincarnation theory explains it. Whatever a person has manifested in this life, he had it at birth, from the very beginning, that is, he gained that power in a previous life. Any talent is only the expression of all that was developed in the particular soul. I saw a girl who was six years old in New York City. She could play Bach and Beethoven on the piano and all the difficult music with such ease and perfection that it amazed everyone. She could hardly span the octave and yet she was playing this complicated music with such sensitivity and expression. Her parents were not musicians. How do we explain that? Heredity cannot explain it. But we can explain that theory easily. Because this child was a musician and the soul of this child was a musician in her previous incarnation, and now she has manufactured another form with a little brain. Her brain is not developed enough to understand such music, but the musician is overshadowing the brain and manipulating all these strings of the brain and the nerve cells and producing all this wonderful music. That is the only rational explanation.

Eternal Life

If we deny preexistence of the soul, we cannot explain immortality. Immortality does not mean that it begins at one end and has endless existence on the other. Preexistence explains the continuity of life in the past, and immortality explains the continuity of life in the future. Immortality means eternal life. You cannot accept one half and deny the other half, because each would be incomplete. So the complete soul-life means eternal past and eternal future. The soul was never born and never created out of nothing. It is the grandest theory and it is the most satisfactory one. It is comforting that we have not come into existence out of nothing, but we have everything in the beginning.

If we are the images of God, then we possess all the powers. God was not a substance that came into existence suddenly, like a mushroom, but He is eternal, and naturally our soul-life must be as eternal as God's life. In fact, we are parts and parcels of God. If we understand how grand and beautiful we are, we do not have to accept the idea that we will no longer live after death. But, on the contrary, we can say that as long as we have desires that need to be fulfilled on this human plane we will come back here. If our desires change, we will go to other planes of existence. For instance, if I have a desire to become an artist like Michelangelo and if in this lifetime I cannot reach that goal that desire will have to be fulfilled. Nothing will stop it because this desire will bring me back to the proper environments where I will gravitate and then begin from childhood with a tendency to become an artist. Nothing can stop me and I will continue until I become a master artist. That is the law of nature. So whatever desires we posses, if those desires are strong, then those desires will shape our future and create our destiny. This idea has been given in the *Bhagavad Gītā:*

> Whatsoever desire is very strong during the lifetime becomes predominant at the time of death, and that desire molds the creation of the subtle body of the individual and that determines the future of the individual. (VIII:6)

We make our future by our thoughts and desires. If we desire to be great politicians, saviors, or artists we will become that which we desire. In fact, we live in eternity. Do not despair. If we cannot be great artists in this life, there are hundreds of lives to come until we satisfy that desire. And when one set of desires is fulfilled others will spring up. As each individual soul possesses infinite potentialities and possibilities, so it can express an infinite variety of manifestations because we are all eternal, and are parts of the Infinite.

The idea of preexistence and reincarnation has settled the questions and solved the problems of life and death amongst the ancient philosophers like Plato, Pythagoras, and the Neo-Platonists and also among poets like Wordsworth, Tennyson, Walt Whitman, and others. Walt Whitman said: "As to you Life, I reckon you are the leavings of many deaths. No doubt I have died myself ten thousand times before."

He learned this truth through the study of Vedanta, just as Emerson learned the belief in reincarnation from the study of Vedanta. It is also true that there is no other philosophy that manifests this idea as strongly as Vedanta does. Of course, Plato and Pythagoras got their ideas through Persia and Egypt from India. The Hindus understood the secret of this law of preexistence and reincarnation even at the dawn of human civilization on the earth. That idea spread among the early Christians also until the time of Justinian, who anathematized all those that believed in this idea, in the Council of Constantinople in 638 AD. He said, "Whoever believes in this wonderful doctrine of preexistence of the soul, let him be anathema."

The churches from that time have not accepted it, although it is in the Old and in the New Testament. It was threatening to their scheme of salvation. But outside of the orthodox people, there are millions of people in the world, who find comfort in it like the Buddhists, Japanese, Hindus, and poets and thinkers of all countries. Therefore it is the rational solution and explains all the causes of inequalities and diversities and the appearance of prodigies. Heredity or the theory of one birth, as explained by the orthodox theologians, does not explain or solve the problem of life.

Now there may be persons who cannot accept this theory of preexistence and reincarnation because they cannot remember their former lives. They say, well, if we existed before, why do we not remember what we did? But do you remember what you did in your childhood? Would you say you did not exist then, because you cannot remember? Certainly not. The details of all the experiences that you have gone through as a child you have now forgotten, but the knowledge that you have gathered through those experiences, is part and parcel of your being and that has shaped you as you are. Memory is of short duration and is sometimes strong and sometimes weak....

Vedanta philosophy tells us not to think of the past but to mold our present, so that we can improve our future. Of course, there is a method by which we can remember our past, because all the experiences that we have gained during our life are stored up in our subconscious mind where all these impressions are pigeonholed. We can bring them out, if we focus our intelligence upon any particular branch of the experience that we like to remember. There are also cases such as two lovers who fall in love at the first sight. There we can explain that these souls loved before, and naturally they remember that and feel as if they had met each other. And what is love? Love does not mean passion. It means the attraction of two souls. It is not on the physical plane, but it must be on the soul-plane, because love is God. It is the divine force; it is the divine attraction of two souls. If there be pure love between any man and woman, that pure love will continue to hold them together even after the death of the body. But at the same time we must remember that love must be mutual. If the husband loves the wife and the wife loves the husband truly and unselfishly then that love is mutual. But if you love somebody and that somebody loves somebody else, then there would be no meeting until both were attracted to each other. Therefore it is necessary to develop that kind of love which would be mutual and then that love will hold the lover and the beloved together throughout eternity. There is no separation in it. So you need not be afraid of being separated from your beloved, and if your beloved be born again, after you go from this plane, you will be born again and you will come together unexpectedly and enjoy the beautiful effects of pure and divine love.

Therefore, if we study this carefully, we see that preexisteance and reincarnation go hand in hand and they explain all the difficulties and problems of life and death as well as of existence and also that we are the creators of our own destiny. Our present life is the result of our past, and our future will be the result of our present. Whether we remember or not, that does not make any difference. We are subject to this eternal law. There are souls who can remember; those who have risen to the height of spiritual consciousness can see their past and future just as if it were eternally present. Therefore Lord Krishna said to Arjuna:

> Oh Arjuna, both you and I have passed through many births. You know them not, but I remember them all. (*Bhagavad Gītā*: IV:5)

So anyone who reaches that state of super-consciousness develops a vision. By developing that vision one can see the past and the future and remember all the experiences that one has gone through and all the experiences that one will still go through. And when we understand that life is eternal, we do not worry about our failures, successes, diseases, or sufferings on this earthly plane. Our life on this plane is only for a short time, but from the standpoint of eternal life we are never born and we are never going to die, because we are birthless, deathless, eternal, immortal. We are part and parcel of the infinite spirit, which is worshiped under different names.

PART TWO

The Law of Karma

I know not what the future holds,
but I know who holds the future.

E. Stanley Jones

Blame no one for your faults, stand upon your own feet, and take the whole responsibility upon yourselves. Say to yourself, "This misery that I am suffering is of my own doing, and that very thing proves that it will have to be undone by me alone." That which I created, I can demolish; that which is created by someone else I shall never be able to destroy. Therefore, stand up, be bold, and be strong. Take the whole responsibility on your own shoulders, and know that you are the creator of your own destiny.

All the strength and succor you want is within yourselves. Therefore, make your own future. "Let the dead past bury its dead." The infinite future is before you, and you must always remember that each thought, word, and deed lays up a store for you. And that as the bad thoughts and bad works are ready to spring upon you like tigers, so also there is the inspiring hope that the good thoughts and good deeds are ready with the power of a hundred thousand angels to defend you always and forever.

Swami Vivekananda
Life After Death

V

The Law of Karma *in Indian Thought*

by Swami Yatiswarananda

The word karma means not only action, physical and mental, but also reaction — reaction of the mind to external stimuli. The forces generated by actions, good or bad, produce good or bad consequences which affect the doer, that is, one who performs actions in an egocentric way with a view to get results. Thus, the Law of Karma is actually the law of causation. It is the great moral law which in its individual and collective aspect guides the destinies of individuals and society.

Every action produces two kinds of results. One is the cosmic effect which determines our future experiences — happiness or misery. The second effect of karma is individual. Every action leaves behind an impression in the mind called *saṁskāra*. Thousands of such *saṁskāra-s* are stored up in our mind, which get activated again later on as tendencies or *vāsanā-s*. And these subtle impressions determine the course of our future births. This is not as mysterious as we think. If we analyze our own minds, we find that many of our present thoughts had their origin in our childhood. Certain ideas and experiences received in childhood leave deep marks on our minds. As we grow, and as the films of our minds are developed, we are surprised to find how many pictures and ideas we have in our minds. It is like the playing back of a tape-recording. Often we forget the source of some of our tendencies but through introspection we can trace them to our early childhood and even to our previous births. Some of our dreams when analyzed give us a wealth of details about our past; often they point to experiences of past lives.

The Law of Karma has two aspects, the binding one and the freeing one. Karma, when performed with egotism and attachment, binds the soul more and more. Repeated sense enjoyments make previous impressions stronger and drag the person down to the plane of birth and death. But when karma is done with detachment, as a service to the Lord or purely for the welfare of others, it leads to the liberation of the soul. Detachment of the self can be practiced either through constant self-analysis and alertness, or by constant self-surrender to the Divine. When this is done, no new impressions are created and the old ones do not become stronger. Gradually, all the previous impressions of the mind lose their sway over us. This is called the purification of the mind and it is achieved through karma. Thus karma in itself is not bad, it is the way we do it that determines whether it binds us or not.

The Ultimate Cause

All schools of philosophy in India, whether they are theistic or non-theistic, accept the Law of Karma. But the real question is this: Has the Supreme Being or God any connection with the working of this law? Is there a divine Will behind its operation? A story is told of the great French astronomer and mathematician Laplace who laid the foundation of the theory of "Spherical Harmonics." When he presented his famous book *The Celestial Mechanism* to Napoleon, the Emperor asked him about the place of God in his system. The astronomer quietly replied, "Sir, I have done without that hypothesis." Well, to many scientists God is just a hypothesis, which one can dispense with.

Agnosticism or atheism, ignoring or denying the existence of God, has become somewhat fashionable nowadays with a class of superficial thinkers in various fields like science, economics, politics, and so on. This theory is often flaunted as modern, and many youngsters in India are taking to it more and more. Now, when we try to understand the minds of such people, we find that they are not yet mature. They lack the earnestness or capacity to go deep down into their own minds or even to think deeply about any subject. In fact, it is not an easy thing to think deeply. This requires a disciplined mind. Most of the so-called modern materialists want only to repeat the ideas of some others and follow them blindly.

I am reminded of a story. A teacher was teaching arithmetic to small children. She set a problem for them to solve. "I have twelve sheep," she said, "Six of them jump the fence and run away. How many would be left?" Most of the boys answered, "Six." But a farmer's boy quietly said, "None would be left." When the teacher questioned him about it, the boy said, "Ma'am, you may know arithmetic but I know the ways of sheep." Here is a lesson for us. We should not follow others blindly like sheep. As a scientist put it: "For most people, the spinal cord is enough; the brain is something redundant." That means most people lead instinctive, impulsive lives. Very few people really think and consciously guide their own lives.

There is nothing modern about materialism. In ancient India we had a school of thinkers called the *Cārvāka-s*. They denied the existence of God, the soul, and immortality, and held that the purpose of life was gross sense enjoyment. They never seemed to have had much influence on the people. But have the old *Cārvāka-s* disappeared? They are hiding in many of us, who profess religion but in actual life follow the materialist conception of life....

Of all the various systems of philosophy in India, Vedanta alone has given paramount importance to God and has triumphed and flourished. All those schools that denied the existence of God have either disappeared from its soil or have merged in the mainstream of Vedanta.

We hear about gigantic machines and most intricate computers and are very much impressed by their efficient work. But we forget that there are intelligent beings that have discovered these and are operating them. In the same way, though this infinite and mysterious universe seems to be going all by itself, it is guided by a cosmic Being who is of the nature of supreme Intelligence and is immanent in all beings. You sow a seed in the ground and pour some water. The seed germinates and grows. Are we to believe that there is a personal deity, Narayana or Siva, sitting somewhere out there in *Vaikuntha* or *Kailāsa* directing the growth of the seed? There is divinity hidden in all beings. It is this immanent divine Principle that controls all life movements. Some of the Western philosophers also speak of an immanent cosmic Will. The Law of Karma is under the guidance of the divine Will. But God Himself is beyond its control. He is ever free and ever pure and is of the nature of Supreme Consciousness and Bliss.

Vedanta further believes that man need not always go on performing actions. Actions are to be performed only as long as the soul is not awakened to the inner Reality. When the soul realizes its real nature to be the same as the Divine, it too goes beyond the operation of the Law of Karma; it becomes free. This final freedom from the cycle of birth and death is the goal of life, according to Vedanta. In the *Muṇḍaka Upaniṣad* we find a beautiful imagery illustrating this point. There are two birds of beautiful plumage dwelling on the same tree. One bird eats the fruits of the tree — some bitter, some sweet — while the other, sitting at the top of the tree, simply looks on, being perfectly unattached. After some time the lower bird looks up, realizes its oneness with the upper bird and stops eating, and also attains supreme peace. The lower bird stands for the *jīva,* the individual soul, who is bound by karma and enjoys and suffers repeatedly. But when it realizes its oneness with the Supreme Spirit, represented by the upper bird, it becomes free from all attachments and limitations and gets established in its own glory.[1]

It is not necessary to remain bound by the Law of Karma and be ground by its wheel. There is a way to free oneself from its painful cogs. In the *Bhagavad Gītā*, Krishna teaches Arjuna the direct path to free himself from the bondage of karma, "Give up all your *dharma* and *adharma* and surrender yourself to Me unconditionally I will save you from all bondage. Do not grieve."[2] That is the Divine promise to mankind. All the great incarnations have given such a promise to mankind. The difficulty is to have faith in it and surrender oneself whole-heartedly to the Divine.

Footnote:

[1] *Muṇḍaka Upaniṣad*, 3.1.1-2
[2] *Bhagavad Gītā*, 18:66

VI

A Karmic Tale

by Paul Carus

Long, long ago in the days of early Buddhism, India was in a most prosperous condition. The inhabitants of the country were highly civilized, and the great cities were centers of industry, commerce, and learning.

It was in those olden times that Pandu, a wealthy jeweler of the brahmin caste, traveled in a carriage to Varanasi. He was bent on some lucrative banking business, and a slave who attended to the horses accompanied him.

The jeweler was apparently in a hurry to reach his destination, and as the day was exceedingly pleasant, since a heavy thunderstorm had cooled the atmosphere, the horses sped along rapidly.

While proceeding on their journey the travelers overtook a *samana*, as the Buddhist monks were called, and the jeweler observing the venerable appearance of the holy man, thought to himself: "This *samana* looks noble and saintly. Companionship with good men brings luck; should he also be going to Varanasi, I will invite him to ride with me in my carriage."

Having saluted the *samana* the jeweler explained where he was going and at what inn he intended to stay in Varanasi. Learning that the *samana*, whose name was Narada, also was travelling to Varanasi, he asked him to accept a seat in his carriage. "I am obliged to you for your kindness," said the *samana* to Pandu, "for I am quite worn out by the long journey. As I have no possessions in this world, I cannot repay you in money; but it may happen that I can reward you with some spiritual treasure out of the wealth of the information I have received while following Shakyamuni, the Blessed One, the Great Buddha, the Teacher of gods and men."

They traveled together in the carriage and Pandu listened with pleasure to the instructive discourse of Narada. After about an hour's journey, they arrived at a place where the road had been rendered almost impassable by a washout caused by the recent rain, and a farmer's cart heavily laden with rice prevented further progress. The loss of a linchpin had caused one of the wheels to come off, and Devala, the owner of the cart, was busily engaged in repairing the damage. He too, was on his way to Varanasi to sell his rice, and was anxious to reach the city before the dawn the next morning. If he was delayed a day or two longer, the rice merchants might have left town or bought all the stock they needed.

When the jeweler saw that he could not proceed on his way until the farmer's cart was removed, he began to grow angry and ordered Mahaduta, his slave, to push the cart aside, so that his carriage could pass. The farmer remonstrated because being so near the slope of the road, it would jeopardize his cargo; but Pandu would not listen to the farmer and bade his servant overturn the rice-cart and push it aside. Mahaduta, an unusually strong man, who seemed to take delight in the injury of others, obeyed before the *samana* could interfere. The rice was thrown on the wayside, and the farmer's plight was worse than before. The poor farmer began to scold, but when the big, burly Mahaduta raised his fist threateningly, he ceased his remonstrations and only growled his curses in a low undertone.

When Pandu was about to continue his journey, the *samana* jumped out of the carriage and said: "Excuse me, sir, for leaving you here. I am under obligations for your kindness in giving me an hour's ride in your carriage. I was tired when you picked me up on the road, but now, thanks to your courtesy, I am rested, and

recognizing in this farmer an incarnation of one of your ancestors, I cannot repay your kindness better than by assisting him in
his troubles."

Pandu looked at the *samana* in amazement: "That farmer
you say is an incarnation of one of my ancestors? That is impossible!"

"I know," replied the *samana*, "that you are not aware of the
numerous important relations which tie your fate to that of the
farmer; but sometimes the smartest men are spiritually blind. So
I regret that you harm your own interest, and I shall try to protect
you against the wound which you are about to inflict upon yourself."

The wealthy merchant was not accustomed to being repri-
manded, and feeling that the words of the *samana* although ut-
tered with great kindness, contained a stinging reproach, bade
his servant drive on without further delay.

The Jeweler's Purse

The *samana* saluted Devala, the farmer, and began to help him
repair his cart and load up the rice, part of which had been
thrown out. The work proceeded quickly and Devala thought:
"This *samana* must be a holy man; invisible *devas* seem to assist
him. I will ask him how I deserved ill treatment at the hands of
the proud brahmin." And he said, "Venerable Sir, can you tell me
why I suffer an injustice from a man to whom I have never done
any harm?"

The *samana* said: "My dear friend, you do not suffer an injustice but only receive in your present state of existence the
same treatment which you visited upon the jeweler in a former
life. You reap what you have sown, and your fate is the product
of your deeds. Your very existence, such as it is now, is but the
karma of your past lives."

"What is my karma?" asked the farmer.

"A man's karma," replied the *samana*, "consists of all the

deeds both good and evil that he has done in his present and in any prior existence. Your life is a system of many activities, which have originated in the natural process of evolution, and have been transferred from generation to generation. The entire being of every one of us is an accumulation of inherited functions, which are modified by new experiences and deeds. Thus we are what we have done. Our karma constitutes our nature. We are our own creators."

"That may be as you say," rejoined Devala, "but what have I to do with that overbearing brahmin?"

The *samana* replied: "You are in character quite similar to the brahmin, and the Karma that has shaped your destiny differs but little from his. If I am not mistaken in reading your thoughts, I should say that you would, even today, have done the same unto the jeweler if he had been in your place, and if you had such a strong slave at your command as he has."

The farmer confessed that if he had had the power, he would have felt little compunction in treating another man, who had happened to impede his way, in the same way as he had been treated by the brahmin. But thinking of the retribution attendant upon unkind deeds, he resolved to be in the future more considerate with his fellow beings.

The rice was loaded and together they pursued their journey to Varanasi, when suddenly the horse jumped aside. "A snake, a snake!" shouted the farmer. But the *samana* looked closely at the object at which the horse shuddered, jumped out of the cart, and saw that it was a purse full of gold, and the idea struck him: "This money can belong to no one but the wealthy jeweler."

Narada took the purse and found that it contained a goodly sum of gold pieces. Then he said to the farmer: "Now is the time for you to teach the proud jeweler a lesson, and it will rebound to your well-being both in this and in future lives. No revenge is sweeter than the requital of hatred with deeds of good will. I will give you this purse, and when you come to Varanasi drive up to the inn, which I shall point out to you; ask for Pandu, the brahmin, and deliver to him his gold. He will excuse himself for the rudeness with which he treated you, but tell him that you have forgiven him and wish him success in all his undertakings. For, let me tell you, the more successful he is, the better you will prosper; your fate depends in many respects upon his fate. Should the jeweler demand any explanation, send him to the *vihara* where he will find me ready to assist him with advice in case he may feel the need of it."

Business in Varanasi

To corner the market of the necessities of life is not a modern invention. The Old Testament contains the story of Joseph, the poor Hebrew youth who became minister of state, and succeeded with unscrupulous but clever business tricks in cornering the wheat market, so as to force the starved people to sell all their property, their privileges, and even their lives, to Pharaoh. And we read in the Jataka Tales that one of the royal treasurers of Kashi, which is the old name of Varanasi, made his first great success in life by cornering the grass market of the metropolis on the day of the arrival of a horse dealer with five hundred horses.

When Pandu the jeweler, arrived at Varanasi it so happened that a bold speculator had brought about a corner in rice, and Mallika, a rich banker and a business friend of Pandu, was in great distress. On meeting the jeweler he said: "I am a ruined man and can do no business with you unless I can buy a cart of the best rice for the king's table. I have a rival banker in Varanasi who, learning that I had made a contract with the royal treasurer to deliver the rice tomorrow morning, and being desirous to bring about my destruction, has bought up all the rice in Varanasi. The royal treasurer must have received a bribe, for he will not release me from my contract, and tomorrow I shall be a ruined man unless Krishna will send an angel from heaven to help me."

While Mallika was still lamenting the poverty to which his rival would reduce him, Pandu missed his purse. Searching his carriage without being able to find it, he suspected his slave Mahaduta; and calling the police, accused him of theft, and had him bound and cruelly tortured to extort a confession.

The slave in his agonies cried: "I am innocent, let me go, for I cannot stand this pain; I am quite innocent, at least of this crime, and suffer now for other sins. Oh, that I could beg the farmer's pardon whom, for the sake of my master, I wronged without any cause! This torture, I believe is a punishment for my rudeness."

While the officer was still applying the lash to the back of the slave, the farmer arrived at the inn, and to the great astonishment of all concerned, delivered the purse. The slave was at once released from the hands of his torturer. But being dissatisfied with his master, he secretly left and joined a band of robbers in the mountains, who made him their chief on account of his great strength and courage.

When Mallika heard that the farmer had the best rice to sell, fit for delivery to the royal table, he at once bought the whole cartload for treble the price that the farmer had ever received. Pandu, however, glad at heart to have his money restored, rewarded the honest finder, and hastened at once to the *vihara* to receive further explanation from Narada, the *samana*.

Narada said: "I might give you an explanation, but knowing that you are unable to understand a spiritual truth, I prefer to remain silent. Yet I shall give you some advice: Treat every man whom you meet as your own self; serve him as you would demand to be served yourself; for our karma travels; it walks apace though, and the journey is often long. But be it good or evil, finally it will come home to us.

Therefore it is said:

> Slowly but surely deeds
> Home to the doer creep.
> Of kindness sow thy seeds,
> And bliss as harvest reap

"Give me, oh *samana*, the explanation," said the jeweler, "and I shall thereby be better able to follow your advice."

The *samana* said: "Listen then, I will give you the key to the mystery. If you do not understand it, have faith in what I say. Self is an illusion, and he whose mind is bent upon following self, follows a will-o-the-wisp which leads him into the quagmire of sin. The illusion of self is like dust in your eye that blinds your sight and prevents you from recognizing the close relations that obtain between yourself and your fellows, which are even closer than the relations that obtain among the various organs of your body. You must learn to trace the identity of your self in the souls of other beings. Ignorance is the source of sin. There are few that know the truth. Let this motto be your talisman:

> Who injureth others
> Himself hurteth sore;
> Who others assisteth
> Himself helpeth more.
> Let the illusion of self
> From your mind disappear,
> And you'll find the way sure;
> The path will be clear.

"To him whose vision is dimmed by the dust of the world, the spiritual life appears to be cut up into innumerable selves. Thus he will be puzzled in many ways concerning the nature of rebirth, and will be incapable of understanding the import of an all-comprehensive loving-kindness toward all living beings."

The jeweler replied: "Your words, oh venerable Sir, have a deep significance and I shall bear them in mind. I extended a small kindness which caused me no expense whatsoever, to a poor *samana* on my way to Varanasi, and lo! how propitious has been the result! I am deeply in your debt, for without you I should not only have lost my purse, but would have been prevented from doing business in Varanasi which greatly increases my wealth, while if it had been left undone it might have reduced me to a state of wretched poverty. In addition, your thoughtfulness and the arrival of the farmer's rice-cart preserved the prosperity of my friend Mallika, the banker. If all men saw the truth of your maxims, how much better the world would be! Evils would be lessened, and public welfare enhanced."

VII

The Roots of Individual Life

by Swami Chinmayananda

Life can bring forth laughter from some people, but only sobs from others. While some may feel submerged in the ocean of life, others may keep afloat gracefully. For some people life is a burden and they try to run away from it; to others it is an opportunity to be embraced joyfully. Some feel elated or depressed at the bits of life lived separately in meaningless patches; others sense a unity in the apparent diversities. Where do these varied behaviors come from?

We all know that a particular record player plays a particular song because of the distinct pattern of etching on it. The difference between two records, made of the same material and of the same size lies in the difference between the etchings. We may call a record good or bad, love or hate it, all because of the etchings that guide the gramophone needle. The synthetic material with which the records are made deserves neither blame nor praise. When pliable, it takes any pattern of etching that the record manufacturer chooses to give it. A pleasant tune or mere noise all may be recorded with equal ease. Once recorded and fixed, they become entombed, and are resurrected at will by the play of the needle. Etching forms the character of a record, its distinguishing marks, and its reactions to the needle. Similarly, the structure and composition of our mind and intellect are founded upon our own tendencies, *vāsanā-s,* which primarily determine our reactions and responses.

The ancient rishis in their studies observed that every action we perform is the fulfillment of a desire. Our desires are the gross manifestation of the subtler tendencies in us. A desire soon crystallizes in the form of a thought, and the thought helplessly draws us to the appropriate place where this desire can be fulfilled. Our tendencies or *vāsanā-s* are the prime motivators of all our desires and actions. And as long as the desires remain, thoughts will come into our mind creating mental agitation and discontent, which compel us to act, and thus provide a channel for their exhaustion. Therefore, in the mechanism of human action the motivating force behind our desires, thoughts, and actions originate from our innate inclinations and tendencies called *vāsanā-s*. The Sanskrit word *vāsanā* means fragrance. Each individual has *vāsanā-s,* which define his individuality, and are unique to him. In other words, an individual is nothing but a visible form of his *vāsanā-s*. The heterogeneous pattern of human beings is explained by the differences in the texture of their *vāsanā* composition, and no one is exempt from them. Therefore Lord Krishna says in the *Bhagavad Gītā*:

> Even a wise man acts in accordance with his own nature;
> beings will follow their own nature. What can restraint do?
> (III:33)

Even a wise person acts in conformance with his own nature, which is determined by the pattern of his thoughts. Our thoughts are always based on certain ways of thinking, which are designed by the thoughts that we entertained in the past. Even though we know that all of our actions are attempts of the *vāsanā-s* to exhaust themselves in the world, only the realized person is not attached to all his activities and their results. Most of us, however, are in a state of complete delusion and are entirely victimized by our own mental temperaments. Bound by numerous attachments we act selfishly, and such actions have a tendency to create new *vāsanā-s*, which create the impulse to act even more vigorously. Let us take the example of how prints or images are created in a camera. When we load the camera with a piece of plain paper, no image of the object can be made on the paper, no matter how long we keep the lenses open against any well-lit object. However, if the very same sheet of paper is sensitive to light, then even a slight exposure will leave the image of the object upon it. Similarly, a mind "sensitized" with attachments soon gathers images (*vāsanā-s*) during its contacts with the external fields of activity. The resulting egocentric thoughts and actions are the cause of the *vāsanā-s* and generate new *vāsanā-s*. And so this endless chain of sorrow continues. Acharya Shankara says:

> Through the increase of *vāsanā-s* egocentric work increases, and when there is an increase of egocentric work there is an increase of *vāsanā-s* also. Thus transmigration never comes to an end. (*Vivekacūḍāmaṇi*: 313)

Thus our entire personality is maintained and managed by the *vāsanā-s,* and the *vāsanā-s* are generated by our egocentric contacts with the world of objects. In our passionate hunger for sense gratification, when we look for and cling to the sense objects, the sensuous *vāsanā-s* increase. The more the subconscious urges the more agitated the mind; hence, the sense organs cannot remain placid. When we continuously indulge in sense objects, we continue to create similar *vāsanā-s*. This cause and effect chain never ends. And when the body becomes incapable of exhausting all the *vāsanā-s*, we move to yet another body where we again accumulate new *vāsanā-s* and thus the cycle continues resulting in transmigration.

Classifying the Vāsanā-s

According to Vedanta, all of our thoughts and actions, together with our reactions which causes transmigration is called karma. Karma is classified with reference to the past, present, and future. It is of three types: *saṁcita karma, prārabdha karma,* and *āgāmī karma.* The total impressions gained by an individual through all his thoughts and actions are called *saṁcitaṁ*, which means "accumulated." They are accumulated at the unmanifest or the subtlest level of the personality. "The effects of actions performed in millions of previous births and stored up in the form of seeds, which in their turn would give rise to endless cycles of births, are called *saṁcita karma* or accumulated karma." (*Tattva Bodha*)

We are the various "effects" arising from different "causes"; hence, the "causes" being different, the "effects" are also different. Each of our actions from the past had its reaction. Therefore we all have a storehouse of past reactions which forms *saṁcita karma*. At the end of experiencing the "fruits" allotted for this life, we take the next form according to the pattern ordained by the ripened "fruits" in our total *saṁcita karma* called *prārabdha karma.*

> Having caused the birth of this body, the karma that gives results in the form of happiness or misery in this world is called *prārabhda karma*. This karma can only be destroyed by enjoying or suffering it out. Thus, *prārabhda karma* can be exhausted only by reaping or experiencing the fruits thereof. (*Tattva Bodha*)

To explain it more clearly, suppose we have a piece of land divided into plots. In one plot we plant coconut seeds, and in the second, mango seeds. In order to germinate, grow, and yield fruit, each seed will take its own time. Similarly, each of our actions has its own time limit for its fruition. Every action has its own reaction, but certain actions give their reactions immediately, while others provide their reactions only after a long interval. To enjoy or suffer the reactions of the past actions, we need certain experiences, and in order to generate these required experiences we must have a definite "field." This field is our world. Here the "world" means the special inner world in which we live our own inner experiences, even though the external world of objects remains the same for all. The differences in the individual experiences are all due to the presence of the *prārabhda vāsanā*.

> As long as there is the experience of happiness and sorrow, the work of prarabdha is seen to persist. Every result is seen to have a preceding action; there can be no result independent of action. (*Vivekacūḍāmaṇi*: 447)

Śruti (scripture) acknowledges that as long as there is a perception of happiness or sorrow, *prārabdha* persists. The logical reason for this is that without a cause an effect is impossible. We see everyone experiencing joys and sorrows, therefore there must have been cause for these experiences in the past, every result is seen to have a preceding action, as there can be no result independent of action.

If all *prārabdha* ends, then there cannot be any experience of joy or sorrow. It is because of the *prārabdha vāsanā-s* that we have taken this body and express ourselves the way we do. The body moves and acts expressing its powerful *vāsanā-s*, and it will surely die once the *vāsanā-s* are exhausted.

Again, some people misunderstand the real meaning of *prārabdha* when they take the word to mean all their failures and weaknesses. If we were to be guided by this delusion in each of our actions then there would be no room for self-improvement through self-effort. There are some who console themselves by saying, "I have no faith or hope, and it is my *prārabdha*." This is a defeatist mentality, and as long as we entertain and live in this defeatist mentality, we cannot expect any progress.

Understanding the Law of Karma

The Law of Karma is often misunderstood as the Law of Destiny. But there is a lot of difference between the Law of Karma and the Law of Destiny. Had the Law of Karma been the same as the Law of Destiny, the Hindu civilization would have ended long ago, like the Roman or the Egyptian civilizations. The Law of Destiny has a corroding effect upon the human personality, and in a short time renders its followers to be mere ineffectual people. Some of us blame the Creator for all our misfortunes and say that it is all fate. But all of us understand that there is a rhythm in the universe, in that the planets "move" regularly, and the whole world of things and beings behave according to a definite pattern. It is only when we try to fathom our own life that we say that there is no rhythm and logic in it.

But those who really understand and believe in the Law of Karma and live up to it become spiritual giants and dynamic citizens. The Law of Karma is based upon the final conclusion that this life is not an end in itself, but just one of the little incidents in our eternal Existence. We all experience life differently, and our destiny is also different. Had this been the very first and the last of our births, all of us would have a greater uniformity of experiences in life. When we inquire about the cause for the great differences between individual experiences, we conclude that this life is only one in a series of our incarnations. We must have had many incarnations in the past, and many more to come in the future. From birth to death and from death to birth the cycle continues, but we do not appreciate or understand it, because we view life from a limited point of view.

When we think of life as being all that we experience during the interval between our birth and death, we do not see the larger picture. Imagine that there is a large painting on a wall. In order to be able to see the entire picture, we have to distance ourselves to get the entire view. Only then can we appreciate the rhythm of the colors, the beauty of the curves, and so on. Similarly, when we look at our present life with a little more objectivity and detachment we get the correct view of the entire life-span and understand it better, and we no longer think of it as being illogical or unrhythmic. The right way of looking at life is to review life in the concept of time-flow, wherein the future, through the present, is ever becoming the past.

From the seed the tree emerges; the seed is the cause, and the tree is the effect. From cotton the cloth is made; cotton is the cause, and cloth is the effect. Now, in all conceivable examples the *cause* is, like the father of a child, the *anterior*, and the *effect*, like the child, the *posterior*. With reference to time, the father was in existence before the child was born. Cause is therefore that which *was*, and the effect is that which *is*. The past causes the present; the present will therefore cause the future.

The Law of Destiny does not take into account this cause and effect relationship. Thus it is unable to explain to us how, even while we live through the preordained pattern of circumstances, we can have a limited freedom to start fresh from moment to moment. As this idea is not clearly explained in the Law of Destiny, our morale becomes shattered, taking away our enthusiasm and making us dull, inactive individuals.

It is true that the Divine Law gives us a limited freedom. For example, we cannot bend a piece of iron as it is, but suppose we beat the iron, it then becomes pliable and can be made into a chain. Similarly, a cow tied with a rope in the center of a pasture is not free to graze the entire field, but she can move freely within a circle with a radius equal to the length of the rope. In the same way, though we have taken up the body to live a fixed *prārabdha* we can reach the supreme goal of life, which is unlimited freedom. We can achieve this divine goal by living fully and correctly the limited freedom allowed to us from moment to moment.

At every moment we are consciously or unconsciously preparing ourselves for our lives yet to come. *Prārabdha* is caused by actions done in the past. It is the very self-effort of the past. So, if our *prārabdha* has made us sorrowful now, let us perform good actions today so that we can order a happier future for ourselves.

When understood correctly, the Law of Karma is the greatest force of vitality in Indian Philosophy. It makes us architects of our own future. We are not helpless pawns in the hands of a mighty tyrant — God, who, it is wrongly believed has created us to be weak and tearful to lead our lives of limitations and sorrow. If we are weak or sorrowful, it is all because of our own willful actions. In our ignorance we pursued certain negative values, and like a Frankenstein their fruits have come to trouble us in life today.

Freedom from all Karma

How can we attain freedom from all our karma? It is true that the desire-prompted activities of the past leave behind their impressions (*vāsanā-s*), and prompted by which the individualized ego seeks a favorable physical environment where it can fulfill its residual *vāsanā-s*. Hence the ego-center takes an appropriate body and manifests itself under the required environments. The new body is manifest from the actions of the past, and since *prārabdha* is the result of past actions, we can concede that the body is the product of *prārabdha*. Therefore, *prārabdha* belongs to the body. It is the destiny of the gross, subtle, and causal bodies that they should suffer or enjoy, and to do this they should be in a favorable environment. But there is no *prārabdha* for the real Self, as the Self is not a product of any past actions. Therefore, for one who has realized his perfect identity with the supreme infinite Self, there cannot be any *prārabdha*. Therefore Acharya Shankara says:

> The body has been fashioned by *prārabdha*, therefore one can accept that *prārabdha* relates to the body. But it is not reasonable to attribute it to the Self, for the *Ātman* is never the result of any earlier work. (*Vivekacūḍāmaṇi*: 459)

> The *Ātmā* is birthless, eternal and indestructible — such is the explicit declaration of *Śruti*. How can *prārabdha* be attributed to him who lives ever identified with That? (*Vivekacūḍāmaṇi*: 460)

Only as long as one lives identified with one's body, can one accept the workings of *prārabdha*. But a man of Realization never identifies himself with his body. Hence, in his case, the workings of *prārabdha* should be rejected.
(*Vivekacūḍāmaṇi*: 461)

A person of perfection is one who has ended these misconceptions, and he no longer identifies with the physical body. Since he does not identify himself with his physical body, the tragedies and comedies of the body do not affect him. At some particular stage in his life an individual may realize the Truth; as Shankaracharya did at the age of twelve, Vivekananda at twenty-four, and Buddha at forty-two. But this does not mean that the *vāsanā-s* that had started yielding fruits before the auspicious hour of realization will stop yielding fruits after realization. Before realization the individual had already been conceived in his mother's womb and had started his earthly career. The great pilgrimage that has started is, in itself, an expression of the past *vāsanā-s*. The karma that has started to manifest does not end because of Self-knowledge (*jñāna*). Because of its *prārabdha*, the body continues to exist even after realization. The body has to go through all its experiences because of past karma.

That work which was performed before the dawn of Knowledge and because of which this body is conjured up, is not destroyed by Self-knowledge without yielding its fruits, just like an arrow shot at an object. (*Vivekacūḍāmaṇi*: 452)

From the standpoint of the realized person, it is *prārabdha* of the body and so *it* has to live through it. He is not involved in the experiences of the body, and so he does not suffer, only his body suffers. It is the people around him who tend to get involved with it. Irrespective of the involvement of the subject, the *prārabdha* will continue yielding its dues. The arrow that has left the bow must reach its target. After leaving the bow it cannot be withdrawn. We can change its course only before it leaves the bow, once it has left it shall certainly reach the determined target. Similarly, the body is the arrow that has already started from the mother's womb and is now aimed at the tomb. Its journey is from womb to tomb. Having started its career no one can stop it from reaching its target or change its course while en-route.

> Thinking it to be a tiger, if someone shoots an arrow at an object, it does not stop because the object turns out to be a cow; it still pierces it with full force. (*Vivekacūḍāmaṇi*: 453)

A hunter aims his arrow and thinking that there is a tiger shoots at it. As the arrow whizzes towards the target, the hunter recognizes it to be a cow. Now what can he do? By his revised knowledge the arrow does not stop in its flight. Certainly it strikes its target (the cow) with full force. The knowledge that it is not a tiger but only a cow cannot change or modify the direction of the arrow. Similarly, in the past, thinking that we are the body, we let loose many arrows of thoughts and desires, which have brought us much suffering. In the midst of this suffering we may realize the Truth. Even then, once the thoughts have been willed and wished in a particular direction, they do take their course and come to manifest in a given body. The body has to go through the convulsions of enjoyments or sufferings, which cannot be stopped.

At this stage of discussion a sincere student of Vedanta may have a doubt. If even after realization the realized one is still under the clutches of his *prārabdha*, will he not go back to the old ways of living in sense-indulgence? Therefore Acharya Shankara says:

> If it is asserted that there may still be attachment for sense objects because of the momentum of the past *vāsanā-s*, the reply is, "No." For the *vāsanā-s* get weakened when there is realization of oneness with *Brahman*. (*Vivekacūḍāmaṇi*: 444)

In order to drive home the point Acharya Shankara gives an

example in the following stanza, which amplifies the above Vedantic contention.

Can the meritorious or sinful actions that a man has imagined to have performed in a dream take him to heaven or hell, when he wakes up? (*Vivekacūḍāmaṇi*: 449)

Whatever activities have been performed during the dream state of consciousness, irrespective of their merits or demerits, they cannot bear fruit after the individual wakes up. The good actions of the dream cannot give one iota of happiness after waking up nor can the crimes perpetrated in the dream give the consequent sorrow in the waking state. Between the two states of consciousness there cannot be any transaction, for the egos that experience the two states of consciousness are totally different. The waker as the waker is not available in the dream. And the dreamer as the dreamer is not there to experience the waking state. In the same way, the egocentric individuality must have performed innumerable actions in his pilgrimage from one form to another. Yet now in his newly-found experience of the Infinite Consciousness as his own true nature, none of the fruits of actions can ever affect him, because the doer of those actions is no longer available. In other words, the ego has ended.

With this realization, "I am Brahman"; the actions of a hundred crore cycles come to naught, like the actions in the dream on waking up. (*Vivekacūḍāmaṇi*: 448)

Acharya Shankara points out here that there is a total destruction of all *vāsanā-s* that have been hoarded from the past, *saṁcita*, arising from the deep contemplation upon, "I am *Brahman*." By this subjective realization "I am the Supreme Consciousness" all the imprints of the past actions left on our personality become totally eradicated and erased. The *vāsanā-s* accumulated in millions of past lives can no more manifest their influence on the personality of an individual who has realized Truth.

When the teacher says that all the *vāsanā-s* accumulated in the past are destroyed, it means that not only are all the *saṁcita vāsanā-s* destroyed, but also all the *vāsanā-s* that are to mature in future and yield their results, called *āgāmī karma*, are also totally destroyed. On realizing the Self, which is unattached to the activities taking place, the seeker's contact with the past is so completely annihilated that even the immature *vāsanā-s* awaiting expression get totally roasted in the fire of Knowledge.

> Being unattached and indifferent like the sky, one who is realized is never concerned about actions yet to be performed. (*Vivekacūḍāmaṇi*: 450)

When a person of realization acts, he is not affected at all by the *vāsanā-s* yet to mature in the future — the *āgāmī*. Karma is a product of the ego and the ego alone can get its reward or punishment. When the doer of the actions, the vain ego, has been totally sublimated, who is to receive the results? When the ego has ended the results of the karma done by the ego can no longer take effect and therefore no *āgāmī* can function. However, the karmas that have taken effect already, for the experience of which the body of the person of Realization has taken its birth, that is, the *prārabdha*, will continue to function and produce results. This body being the result of the *prārabdha* continues to exist, even after realization until it is exhausted by itself. Thus, the *āgāmī* and *saṁcita* can be eliminated, but not the *prārabdha*. That is, the *prārabdha* of the body, not of the realized individual, for he lives without any identification with it. Summarizing Shankara says:

> *Prārabdha* is very powerful even for the realized person and becomes naught only through the exhaustion of its fruits, while the *saṁcita* and *āgāmī* are destroyed in the fire of perfect Knowledge. But none of the three affects those who have realized *Brahman* and are always identified with it. They are truly the transcendental *Brahman*. (*Vivekacūḍāmaṇi*: 454)

Prārabdha karma is very strong even for those who have attained realization. The *āgāmī* and *saṁcita* can be ended by the experience of the Higher, but *prārabhda* will end only when it has been lived through. Whether a person is a *jñāni* (wise) or an *ajñānī* (ignorant), he has to live through it. There is no escape. A wise person may have a happy smile on his face since he knows that he is not the equipment; an ignorant person unfortunately will make a long face, for he will not have the strength to grin and bear his lot.

VIII

The Path of the Soul

by Swami Vivekananda

According to the Vedantists, when this body dissolves, the vital forces of the person go back to his mind. And the mind becomes dissolved, as it were, into the *prāṇa*, and that *prāṇa* enters into the soul of man. And the soul of the person comes out, clothed, as it were, with what they call the fine body, mental body, or spiritual body, whatever you may want to call it. In this body are the *saṁskāra-s* of the person. What are the *saṁskāra-s*?

This mind is like a lake, and every thought is like a wave upon that lake. Just as in the lake waves rise and then fall down and disappear, so these thought-waves are continually rising in the mind-stuff and then disappearing, but they do not disappear forever. They become finer and finer, but they are all there, ready to start up at another time when called upon to do so. Memory is simply calling back into wave-form some of those thoughts which have gone into that finer state of existence. Thus everything that we have thought, every action that we have done, is lodged in the mind. It is all there in fine form, and when a person dies, the sum total of these impressions is in the mind, which again works upon a little fine material as a medium. The soul, clothed, as it were, with these impressions and the fine body, passes out, and the destiny of the soul is guided by the resultant of all the different forces represented by the different impressions. According to Vedanta, there are three different goals for the soul.

Those that are very spiritual when they die follow the solar rays and reach the solar sphere, through which they reach the lunar sphere, and through that they reach the sphere of lightning, and there they meet with another soul who is already blessed. This super-human being guides the newcomer forward to the highest of all spheres, which is called the *Brahmaloka*, the sphere of *Brahma*. There these souls attain to omniscience and omnipotence, become almost as powerful and all-knowing as God Himself, and, according to the dualists, reside there forever. Or, according to the non-dualists, they become one with the universe at the end of the cycle.

The next class of persons, those who have been doing good work with selfish motives, are carried by the results of their good works to what is called the lunar sphere, where there are various heavens, and there they acquire fine bodies, the bodies of gods. They become gods and live there and enjoy the blessing of heaven for a long period. After that period is finished the old karma is again upon them, and so they fall back again to the earth. They come down through the spheres of air and clouds and all these various regions, and, at last, reach the earth through raindrops. There on the earth they attach themselves to some cereal, which is eventually eaten by some man who is fit to supply them with material to make a new body.

The last class of persons, the wicked, become ghosts or demons, and live somewhere midway between the lunar sphere and this earth. Some try to disturb mankind, some are friendly; and after living there for some time they also fall back to the earth and become animals. After living for some time in an animal body they get released and come back, and become men again and thus get one more chance to work out their salvation.

We see, then, that those who have nearly attained to perfection in whom only very little of impurity remains go to the *Brahmaloka* through the rays of the sun. Those who were a middling sort of people, who did some good work with the idea of going to heaven, go to the heavens in the lunar sphere and there obtain god-bodies, but they have again to become men and so get one more chance to become perfect. Those that are very wicked become ghosts and demons, and then they may have to become animals; after that they become men again and get another chance to perfect themselves.

The Sphere of Karma

This earth is called the *Karma-Bhūmi*, the sphere of karma. Here alone man makes his good or bad karma. When a man wants to go to heaven and does good works for that purpose, he becomes good and does not as such store up any bad karma. He just enjoys the effects of the work he did on earth. But when this good karma is exhausted, there is still the resultant force of the evil karma that he had previously stored up in life and that brings him down again to this earth. In the same way, those that become ghosts remain in that state, not giving rise to fresh karma, but suffer the evil results of their past misdeeds, and later on remain for some time in an animal body without causing any fresh karma. When that period is finished, they too become men again.

The states of reward and punishment due to good and bad karmas are devoid of the force that generates fresh karmas; they have only to be enjoyed or suffered through. If, however, there is an extraordinarily good or an extraordinarily evil karma it bears fruit very quickly. For instance, if a man has been doing many evil things all his life, but does one good act, the result of that good act will immediately appear, but when that result has been gone through, all the evil acts must produce their results also. It is the same with those who do good actions, they will live in god-bodies for some time enjoying the power of gods. But since the general tenor of their lives was not correct they will again have to become men, for when the power of the good actions are finished, the old evil comes up to be worked out. Those who do extraordinarily evil acts have to put on ghost and devil bodies, and when the effect of those evil actions is exhausted, the little good action, which remains associated with them, makes them become men again. The way to *Brahmaloka*, from which there is no more fall or return, is called the *Devayāna*, (the Northern Path) that is, the way to God. The way to heaven is known as *Pitrayāna*, (the Southern Path) that is, the way to the Fathers.

According to Vedanta philosophy, man is therefore the greatest being that is in the universe, and this world the best place to work out his karma, because only herein is the greatest and the best chance for him to become perfect. Angels or gods, whatever you may call them, have all to become men, if they want to become perfect. This human life is therefore a great gift, a wonderful opportunity to perfect ourselves.

IX

Karma: The Heart is our Garden

by Jack Kornfield

We are called upon to act night and day, alone or in community, in wonderful circumstances or confronting difficulties. How can we put our inner understanding into practice, and how can we know when our actions are wise? The key to wise action is an understanding of karma.

Karma has become a common word in our language. There are many examples of this. We say, "It's his karma," or, "He'll get his karma." I even heard an ad on the radio for an automobile dealership that was selling cars in Berkeley at a low price last season because, they said, it was their karma to do so, and: "It's your karma to come in and get one of these good deals." One local paper even advertised a $15.95 service to ensure better karma and more money in the next life, "The Reincarnation Next Lifetime Guarantee" (Guaranteed Wealth or Your Money Back). This is the level to which the idea and use of the word karma has deteriorated in our culture.

The *Avatamsaka Sūtra* is the Buddhist text that describes the laws that govern the thousands of possible realms of the universe — realms of pleasure and realms of pain, realms created by fire, by water, by metal, by clouds, or even by flowers. Each universe, the *Sūtra* tells us, follows the same basic law: In each of these realms if you plant a mango seed, you get a mango tree, and if you plant an apple seed, you will get an apple tree. It is so in every realm that exists in the world of creative phenomena.

The Law of Karma describes the way that cause and effect govern the patterns that repeat themselves throughout all life. Karma means that nothing arises by itself. Every experience is conditioned by that which precedes it. Thus our life is a series of interrelated patterns. The Buddhists say that understanding this is enough to live wisely in the world.

Karma exists at many different levels. Its patterns govern the large forms of the universe, such as the gravitational forces of galaxies, and the smallest, subtlest ways that our human choices affect our moment-to-moment state of mind. At the level of physical life, for example, if one looks at an oak tree, one can see "oak tree" manifesting in several different stages of life's patterns. In one stage of the oak tree pattern, an oak tree exists as an acorn; at a subsequent stage it exists as a sapling, in another stage as a large tree, and in yet another, as the green acorn growing on that large tree. Strictly speaking, there is no such thing as a definitive "oak tree." There is only the oak tree pattern through which certain elements follow the cyclical Law of Karma: a particular arrangement of water, minerals, and the energy of sunlight that changes it from acorn to sapling to large tree over and over again.

The tendencies and habits of our mind are similarly karmic patterns that we repeat over and over, like the acorn and the oak tree. When the Buddha spoke of this, he asked, "Which do you think is larger, the highest mountain on earth or the pile of bones that represents the lives that you have lived over and over in every realm governed by the patterns of your own karma? Greater, my friends, is the pile of bones than the highest mountain on earth."

We live in a sea of conditioning patterns that we repeat over and over, yet we rarely notice this process. We can understand the workings of karma in our lives most clearly by looking at this process of cause and effect in our ordinary activities and by observing how the repetitive patterns of our own mind affect our behavior. For instance, being born in a certain culture at a certain time, we learn certain habit patterns. If we are born into a taciturn fishing culture, we learn to be silent. If we grow up in a more expressive Mediterranean culture, we may express our feelings with gestures and loud talk. Our social karma — parental, school, and linguistic conditioning — creates whole patterns of consciousness that determine the way we experience reality and the way we express ourselves.

These patterns and tendencies are often much stronger than our conscious intentions. Whatever our circumstances, it is old habits that will create the way we live. I remember visiting my grandmother in an apartment building for seniors. Life there was quiet and sedentary for most residents. The only place where anything happened was in the lobby, and interested residents would go there to watch who came in and went out. In the lobby, there were two groups of people. One group regularly sat there enjoying themselves. They played cards, they said hello to everyone who came by. They had a pleasant and friendly relationship with one another and with the circumstances around them. In another part of the lobby were people who liked to complain. For them there was something wrong with everyone who came through the door. In between visitors they complained, "Did you taste the terrible food they served us today?" "Did you see what they did to the bulletin board?" "Have you heard what they're doing with our rent?" "Do you know what my son said the last time he was here?" This was a whole group of people whose main relation to life was to complain about it. Each group brought to the building a pattern they had lived with for many years.

Long-repeated circumstances and mental attitudes become the condition for what we call "personality." When Lama Trungpa Rinpoche was asked what was reborn in our next lives, he joked, "Your bad habits." Our personalities become conditioned according to past causes. Sometimes this is apparent, but very often habits that stem from the distant and unremembered past go unnoticed.

Primary Conditionings

In Buddhist psychology, the karmic conditioning of our personality is categorized according to three basic unconscious forces and automatic tendencies of our mind. There are *desire types,* whose most frequent states of mind are associated with grasping, with wanting, not having enough. There are *aversion types,* whose most common state of mind is to push away the world through judgment, dislike, aversion, and hatred. Then there are the *confused types,* whose most fundamental states are lethargy, delusion, and disconnection, not knowing what to do about things.

You can test which type predominates in you by observing how you typically enter a room. If your conditioning is most strongly that of desire and wanting, you will tend to look around a room and see what you like about it, what you can get, you will see what you are attracted to; you will notice what is beautiful; you will appreciate a beautiful flower arrangement; you will like the way certain people are dressed; you will find someone sexually interesting or imagine that others would be stimulating people to know. If you are an aversion type, you tend to enter a room and, instead of first seeing what you want, you see what is wrong: "It's too loud. I don't like the wallpaper. People aren't dressed right. I don't like the way the whole thing is organized." If you are a confused personality, you may walk into a room, look around, and not know how to relate, wondering, "What is going on here? How do I fit in? What am I supposed to do?"

This primary conditioning is actually a very powerful process. It grows into the forces that bring whole societies into war, create racism, and drive the lives of many around us. When we first encounter in ourselves the forces of desire and aversion, of greed and hatred, we might think that they are harmless, a bit of wanting, of dislike, a bit of confusion. However, as we observe our conditioning, we see that fear, grasping, and avoidance are in fact so compelling that they govern many aspects of our personality. Through observing these forces we can see how the patterns of karma operate.

When we begin to look closely at our personalities in meditation, our first impulse is often to try to get rid of our old habits and defenses. Initially most people find their own personality difficult, unpleasant, and even unsavory. The same thing can happen when we look at the human body. It is beautiful at the right distance, at the right age, and in the right light, but the closer we look, the more flawed it becomes. When we see this, we try dieting, jogging, skin care, exercise, and a vacation to improve our body. But even though these may be beneficial, we are still basically stuck with the body we were born with. Personalities are even more difficult to alter than our bodies, but the purpose of spiritual life is not to get rid of our personality. Some of it was there when we were born, some has been conditioned by our life and culture, and no matter what, we can't do without it. On this earth we all have a body and a personality.

Our task is to learn about this very body and mind and awaken in the midst of it. Understanding the play of karma is one aspect of awakening. If we are not aware, our life will simply follow the pattern of our past habits over and over. But if we can awaken, we can make conscious choices in how we respond to the circumstances of our life. Our conscious response will then create our future karma. We may or may not be able to change our outer circumstances, but with awareness we can always change our inner attitude, and this is enough to transform our life. Even in the worst external circumstances, we can choose whether we meet life from fear and hatred or with compassion and understanding.

Transforming the patterns of our life is always done in our heart. To understand how to work with the karmic patterns in our life, we must see that karma has two distinct aspects — that which is the result of our past and that karma which our present responses are creating for our future. We receive the results of past action; this we cannot change. But as we respond in the present, we also create new karma. We sow the karmic seeds for new results. The word *karma* in Sanskrit is usually paired with another word, *vipāka* — *karma vipāka*. *Karma* means "action," and *vipāka* means "result."

In dealing with each moment of our experience, we use either skillful (awakened) or unskillful (unconscious) means. Unskillful responses such as grasping, aversion, and confusion all inevitably create more suffering and painful karma; skillful responses, based on awareness, love, and openness, will inevitably lead to well-being and happiness. Through skillful means, we can create new patterns that transform our life. Even the powerful patterns based on grasping, aversion, and delusion have within them the seeds of skillful responses. Desire for pleasure can be changed into a natural and compassionate action that brings beauty into the society and world around us. The judgmental-aversion temperament can, through awareness, become transformed into what is called *discriminating wisdom:* a clarity associated with compassion, a wisdom that sees clearly through all the delusions of the world, and uses the clarity of truth to help and heal. Even confusion and the tendency to be disconnected from life can be transformed into a wise and spacious equanimity, a wise and compassionate balance that embraces all things with peace and understanding.

Traditionally, karma has often been discussed in Buddhist teachings in terms of death and rebirth. The Buddha told of a vision on the night of his enlightenment in which he saw thousands of his own past lives, as well as those of many other beings, all dying and being reborn according to the lawful karmic results of their past actions. But we do not need to see with Buddha's vision to understand karma. The same karmic laws he described act in our lives from moment to moment. We can see how death and birth take place each day. Each day we are born into new circumstances and experiences as if it were a new life. In fact, this happens in each moment. We die every moment and we are reborn the next.

It is taught that there are four kinds of karma at the moment of death, or in any moment of transition: *weighty karma, proximate karma, habitual karma,* and *random karma.* Each represents a stronger karmic tendency than the one that follows it. The traditional image used to explain this is one of cows in a field when the gate is opened. Weighty karma is like a bull. It is the force from the most powerful good or bad deeds we have done. If a bull is there and you open the gate, the bull always goes through first. Proximate karma is the cow that is nearest the gate. This refers to the state of mind that is present at the moment of transition. If the gate is open and there is no bull present, the cow that is closest goes through. If no cow is particularly near the gate, habitual karma arises. This is the force of our ordinary habit. Without some strong state of mind present, the cow that usually goes first will go through the gate first. Finally, random karma arises if there is no strong habit operating. If no stronger force arises, our karma will be the random result of any number of past conditions.

As each action (or birth) arises, there are forces that sustain it and forces that finally bring it to an end. These karmic forces are described by the image of a garden. The seed that is planted is the *causative karma.* Fertilizing and watering the seed, taking care of the plants, is called *sustaining karma.* When difficulties arise, this is *counteractive karma* portrayed by a drought: even if we plant a viable seed and fertilize it, if there is no water, it will wither away. Then finally, *destructive karma* is like fire or gophers in the garden, which burn it or eat it all up.

This is the nature of life in every realm, in every creative circumstance. One condition follows another, yet all of this is subject to change. The karma of our outer circumstances can change with the flick of a horse's tail. In any day, great good fortune or death can come to any one of us.

The Power of Intention

What brings the karmic result from the patterns of our actions is not our action alone. As we *intend* and then act, we create karma: so another key to understanding the creation of karma is becoming aware of *intention*. The heart is our garden, and along with each action there is an intention that is planted like a seed. The result of the patterns of our karma is the fruit of these seeds.

For example, we can use a sharp knife to cut someone, and if our intention is to do harm, we will be murderers. This leads to certain karmic results. We can perform an almost identical action, using a sharp knife to cut someone, but if we are surgeons, the intention is to heal and save a life. The action is the same, yet depending on its purpose or intention, it can be either a terrible act or a compassionate act.

We can study the power of intention to create karma in our day-to-day life. We can start by paying attention to our many actions that arise throughout the day in response to problems. In an automatic way, we may ignore difficult circumstances or respond critically or harshly. We may try to protect or defend our own way. In all of these cases, the intention in our heart will be bound up with grasping, aversion, or delusion, creating a karma of suffering in the future that will bring back an equivalent response.

When these difficult circumstances arise in our life, if we instead bring to them the desire to understand, to learn, to let go, or to bring harmony and create peace, we will speak and act with a different intention. Our actions might be very similar, our words might be similar, but if our intention is to create peace or bring harmony, it will create a very different kind of karmic result. This is easy to see in close business or personal relationships. We can say the same sentence to our partner or friend, and if the unspoken spirit in saying it is, "I love you and I want us to understand what is going on," we will get one kind of response. If we say the same thing with an underlying attitude of blame, defense, and criticism, with the slightest tone of, "What's wrong with you?" it will create a whole different direction in the conversation and could easily escalate into a fight.

Two short dialogues from *Do I Have to Give Up Me to Be Loved by You* by psychologists Jordan and Margaret Paul illustrate this.

DIALOGUE NO. 1:
JIM: (distant, voice slightly hard) "What's wrong? . . ."
MARY: "Nothing."
Jim then plunks himself down in front of the TV and nothing more is said. The distance between them continues, even widens.

DIALOGUE NO. 2:
JIM: (genuinely soft and curious) "You seem upset. What's wrong?"
MARY: (still closed and hard) "Nothing."
JIM: "Look, hon, I hate this distance. It makes me feel awful. Have I done anything that hurts you?"
MARY: (angry and accusing) "Yes. How come you told Sam and Annie we'd go out with them Saturday and you never even asked me or told me about it?..."
JIM: "Mary, I'd like to talk about this but it's hard to understand what the problem is when you're yelling at me. Do you think we could just talk about it for a while?"
MARY: "Yes, I guess we do need to talk about it."

The intention or attitude that we bring to each situation of life determines the kind of karma that we create. Day to day, moment to moment, we can begin to see the creation of the patterns of karma based on the intentions in our heart. When we pay attention, it becomes possible to become more aware of our intentions and the state of our heart as they arise in conjunction with the actions and speech that are our responses. Usually we are unconscious of them.

For example, we may decide to stop smoking cigarettes, then partway through the day the desire to have a cigarette may arise and we find ourselves reaching in our pocket, pulling out a pack, taking out a cigarette, lighting it up to inhale. All of a sudden we wake up and remember, "Oh, I was going to stop smoking." While on automatic pilot and without awareness, we went through all of the habitual motions of reaching for a cigarette and lighting it. It is not possible to change the patterns of our behavior or create new karmic conditions until we become present and awake at the *beginning* of the action. Otherwise it has already happened. As the old saying goes, "This is like closing the door after the horse has left the barn."

The development of awareness in meditation allows us to become mindful enough or conscious enough to recognize our heart and intentions as we go through the day. We can be aware of the different states of fear, wanting, confusion, jealousy, and anger. We can know when forgiveness or love or generosity is connected with our actions. When we know what state is in our heart, we can begin to have a choice about the patterns or conditions we will follow, and the kind of karma that we create.

Try working with this kind of awareness in your life. Practice it with your speech. Pay very careful attention and notice the state of your heart, the intention, as you speak about even the smallest matter. Is your intention to be protected, to grasp, to defend yourself? Is your intention to open out of concern, compassion, or love? Once you've noticed the intention, then become aware of the response elicited. Even if it is a difficult response, stay with the skillful intention repeatedly for a while and observe the kinds of responses it brings.

If your intention was unskillful or unkind, try changing it and see what happens after a while. At first you may only experience the results of your previously defensive attitude. But persist in your good intention and observe the kinds of responses it eventually elicits. To understand how karma works you need only look at your most personal relationships or your simplest interactions. You can pick a specific relationship or a specific place and experiment there. Try responding only when your heart is open and kind. When you don't feel this way, wait and let the difficult feelings pass. As the Buddha instructed, let your speech and actions arise gently, with kindly intent, in due season, and to their benefit. As you cultivate kind and skillful intention, you can then practice it at the gas station or the supermarket, in the workplace, or in traffic. The intention that we bring creates the pattern that results.

Changing the World by Changing Ourselves

As we become more aware of our own intention and action, karma shows itself to us more clearly. Karmic fruit even seems to come more quickly, maybe simply because we notice it. As we pay attention, the fruit of whatever we do, both skillfully and unskillfully, seems to manifest more quickly. As we study this law of cause and effect we will see that whenever we or someone else acts in a way that is based on grasping, hatred, prejudice, judgment, or delusion, the results will inevitably bring some suffering. We begin to see how those who harm us also create inevitable suffering for themselves. It makes us want to pay closer attention, and as we observe the law of cause and effect we can see directly the skillful and unskillful states in our own heart.

Attention to karma shows us how lives are shaped by the intention in the heart. When asked to explain the Law of Karma in the simplest way, Ruth Denison, a well-known *vipassana* teacher, put it this way: "Karma means you don't get away with 'nothin.'" Every day we are sowing the seeds of karma. There's only one place where we can exercise any influence on karma, and that is in the intention of our actions. In fact, there is only one person's karma that we can change in the whole world — our own. But what we do with our heart affects the whole world. If we can untie the karmic knots in our own heart, because we are all interconnected, we inevitably bring healing for the karma of another. As one ex-prisoner of war said when visiting a fellow survivor, "Have you forgiven those who imprisoned you yet?" The survivor said, "No, I haven't. Never." The first veteran said, "Then somehow they still have you in prison."

When my wife and I were traveling in India some years ago, she had a very painful vision of one of her brothers dying. At first I thought it was part of a death-rebirth process in her meditation. The following day she had a second vision of her brother as a spirit guide, coming along with two Native Americans to offer her support and guidance. About one week later a telegram arrived at the ashram where we were staying on Mount Abu in Rajasthan. Sadly, it told my wife that her brother had in fact died in the fashion that she had seen in her vision. The telegram was dated the day she had her vision. How could she see her brother's death halfway around the world? She could because we are all connected. And because this is so, changing one heart affects all of our hearts, and the karma of all the world.

At one retreat I taught some years ago, a woman was wrestling with the painful results of early abuse in her life. She'd been angry, depressed, and grieving for many years. She had worked in therapy and meditation through a long process to heal these wounds. Finally in this retreat she came to a place of forgiveness for the person who had abused her. She wept with deep forgiveness, not for the act, which can never be condoned, but because she no longer wished to carry the bitterness and hatred in her heart.

She left the retreat and returned home and found a letter waiting in her mailbox. It had been written by the man who had abused her, and with whom she had no contact for fifteen years. While in many other cases, abusers will deny their actions to the last, in spite of forgiveness, something had changed this man's mind. He wrote, "For some reason I felt compelled to write to you. I've been thinking about you so much this week. I know I caused you great harm and suffering and brought great suffering on myself as well. But I simply want to ask your forgiveness. I don't know what else I can say." Then she looked at the date at the top of the letter. It was written the same day that she had completed her inner work of forgiveness.

There's a famous Hindu story of two kingdoms that were each being governed in the name of Krishna. Looking down from heaven, Lord Krishna decided to visit them and see what was being done in his name. So he went and appeared before the court of one king. This king was known to be wicked, cruel, miserly, and jealous. Lord Krishna appeared in his court in a blaze of celestial light. The king bowed to him and said, "Lord Krishna, you've come to visit." Krishna said, "Yes. I wish to give you a task. I would like you to travel throughout the provinces of your kingdom and see if you can find one person who is truly good." This king went out through all his provinces. He talked to high castes and low castes, to priests and farmers, to artisans and healers. Finally he came back to his throne room and waited for Lord Krishna to reappear. When Lord Krishna arrived, he bowed down and said, "My Lord, I've done your bidding. I've gone from low to high throughout my kingdom, but I have not found one truly good person. Though some of them performed many good deeds, when I got to know each person, even their best actions ended up being selfish, self-interested, conniving, or deluded. Not a single good person could I find."

Then Lord Krishna went to the other court ruled by a famous queen named Dhammaraja. This queen was known to be kind, gracious, loving, and generous. Here again Lord Krishna set her to a task. "I would like you to go throughout your kingdom and find one truly evil person for me." So Queen Dhammaraja went through her provinces speaking to low castes and high castes, farmers, carpenters, nurses, and priests. After a long search she returned to her court, whereupon Lord Krishna reappeared. She bowed and said, "My Lord, I have done as you asked, but I have failed my task. I have gone throughout the land, and I've seen many people who act unskillfully, who are misguided, and act in ways that create suffering. Yet when I really listened, not one truly evil person could I find, only those who are misguided. Their actions always came from fear, delusion, and misunderstanding."

In both kingdoms the circumstances of life were governed by the spirit of the rulers, and what they encountered was a reflection of their heart. As we pay attention and understand our own heart and grow in the skillful responses of wisdom and compassion, we do our part to make the whole of the earth peaceful. Through our work and creativity, we can bring about beneficial circumstances outwardly in our life. However, most of the great things that happen to us, where we are born, when we die, the great changes that sweep our lives and the world around us, are the result of ancient and powerful karmic patterns. These we cannot change. They come to us like the wind and the weather. The only weather forecast that we can guarantee is that conditions will continue to change.

Creating our Future

In understanding karma, we must answer a simple question: How do we relate to these changing conditions? What type of universe we create, what we choose to plant, what we bring forth in the garden of our heart will create our future. The Buddha begins his teachings in the great *Dhammapada* by saying:

We are what we think.
All that we are arises with our thoughts.
With our thoughts we make the world.
Speak or act with an impure mind
And trouble will follow you
As the wheel follows the ox that draws the cart.
We are what we think
All that we are arises with our thoughts.
With our thoughts we make the world.
Speak or act with a pure mind
And happiness will follow you
As your shadow, unshakable.

In the long run we posses nothing on this earth, not even our own body. But through our intentions we can shape or direct the patterns of our heart and mind. We can plant seeds in our heart that will create the kind of kingdom the world will be, whether it be wicked and evil or good and compassionate. Through simple awareness of our intention from moment to moment, we can plant a splendid garden, we can create patterns of well-being and happiness that last far beyond our personalities and our limited life.

Vipassana teacher Sylvia Boorstein illustrates this power with a story of a good friend, a famous doctor who for many years had served as president of the American Psychiatric Association. He was known as a gentleman, a man of integrity and kindness, who brought great joy to everything in his life. He always offered a deep respect to his patients and colleagues. After he retired and grew older, he started to become senile. He lost his memory and his ability to recognize people. He still lived at home, and his wife helped take care of him. Being longtime friends, Sylvia and her husband Seymour, who is also a psychiatrist, were invited to his home for dinner one evening. It had been some time since they had last seen him, and they wondered if his senility had increased. They arrived at the door with a bottle of wine and rang the doorbell. He opened the door and looked at them with a kind of blank stare that showed no recognition of who they were, even though they had been friends for many years. Then he smiled and said, "I don't know who you are, but whoever you are, please come and enjoy my home." And he offered them the same graciousness with which he had lived for his whole life.

The karmic patterns that we create through our hearts transcend the limitations of time and space. To awaken the heart of compassion and wisdom in a response to all circumstances is to become a Buddha. When we awaken the Buddha within ourselves, we awaken to a universal force of spirit that can bring compassion and understanding to the whole of the world. Gandhi called this power Soul Force. It brings strength when powerful action is needed. It brings tremendous love and forgiveness yet stands and speaks truth as well. It is this power of our heart that brings wisdom and freedom in any circumstance, that brings the kingdom of the spirit alive here on earth.

For Gandhi this spirit was always connected to his heart, always open to listen and ready to respond to the world by sharing the blessings of compassion with all beings.

"Beyond my non-cooperation there is always the keenest desire to cooperate, on the slightest pretext, even with the worst of opponents. To me, a very imperfect mortal is ever in need of God's grace, ever in need of the dharma. No one is beyond redemption."

PART THREE

The Final Freedom

Open your eyes.
Burst your shell.
Spread your wings and fly.

Swami Chinmayananda

It must be distinctly understood that it is no soul that comes and goes, but only the thinking mind of the individual, which makes it appear to do so. On whatever plane the mind happens to act, it creates a body for itself; in the physical world a physical body and in the dream world a dream body which becomes wet with dream rain and sick with dream disease. After the death of the physical body, the mind remains inactive for some time, as in dreamless sleep when it remains worldless and therefore bodiless. But soon it becomes active again in a new world and a new body — the astral — till it assumes another body in what is called a rebirth. But the *jñānī*, the Self-realized person whose mind has already ceased to act, remains unaffected by death. The mind of the *jñānī* has ceased to exist; it has dropped never to rise again to cause births and deaths. The chain of illusion has snapped forever for him. It should now be clear that there is neither real birth, nor real death. It is the mind that creates and maintains the illusion of reality in this process until it is destroyed by Self-realization.

Ramana Maharshi
Be As You Are

X

Is Death the End?

by Swami Nikhilananda

The *Kaṭha Upaniṣad* begins with a question which has troubled man from time immemorial: "There is this doubt about a man when he is dead, some say that he exists, others, that he does not." Evidently skepticism and atheism are as old as human thinking. As man's expanding consciousness became self-conscious he wanted to know about the true nature of himself and the universe. The *Upanishad* discusses the problem through a story containing a dialogue between Nachiketa and Yama, the King of Death.

Nachiketa was the son of Vajasrava, a pious householder, who, at one time, performed a sacrifice. One of the rules of this sacrifice was that the performer should give away all his possessions to priests and other Brahmins in order to enjoy its reward in a heavenly world. Vajasrava, a person of miserly disposition, made a gift of old and decrepit cows, which could no longer drink, eat, calve, or give milk. Nachiketa, an unusual boy, was endowed with many spiritual qualities, such as purity of body and mind, humility, earnestness, reverence and a single-minded devotion. Furthermore, he possessed *śraddhā*, an unwavering faith in the traditions of his religion, and the words of illumined saints without which the pupil absorbs no spiritual instruction. He realized immediately that such an unworthy gift would not only deprive his father of the wished-for-reward but also lead him to a joyless world after death. A dutiful son, he wished to save his father from this disaster, and so asked to whom he was himself to be given away, since he, too, was one of his father's possessions. Twice he asked this question, which his father regarded as rather impudent and to which he gave no reply. When it was repeated for the third time, however, the father lost his temper and said that he would give Nachiketa away to Yama. In other words, he cursed his son to die.

Yama, who is regarded in the Hindu tradition as a highly spiritual being, is the arbiter of man's destiny after death. Endowed with stern self-control, he is not swayed by personal attachment and aversion. He bestows reward and punishment on departed souls as determined by their merit and demerit, holds a high position among the gods, and is extolled for his knowledge of *Brahman*. The wicked tremble before him, but not the virtuous.

Vajasrava, after his hasty disposition of Nachiketa, realized his folly and began to lament the impending death of his son. But Nachiketa reminded his father that in this impermanent world one should never deviate from truth, and cheerfully went to the abode of Death.

When Nachiketa arrived, Yama was away, and for three nights did not greet his guest. When he returned, he was told of Nachiketa's presence by his ministers and they reminded him that not showing hospitality to a guest deprives the host of the fruit of his meritorious actions, as well as of his children and his cattle. Yama therefore approached Nachiketa, paid him due reverence, and invited him to choose three boons in compensation for the three nights during which he had been neglected in his host's house. For the first boon, Nachiketa prayed to Yama to remove his father's worries about his welfare in the abode of Death. This was granted. Next Nachiketa asked about the Fire Sacrifice, which is a rite that brings its performer to *Brahmaloka*, the most exalted of heavenly worlds. Yama explained to Nachiketa, in detail, the technique of the Fire Sacrifice and was delighted to find that his intelligent disciple grasped the rituals correctly. Then he requested Nachiketa to choose the final boon — and it is this that introduces the real theme of this *Upanishad*, namely, the knowledge of the Self.

The Attainment of Self-Knowledge

The relevance of the first two boons to the attainment of Self-knowledge may be briefly discussed. Respect for parents is the basis of a stable family life, whereby all the members find security in the knowledge that one loves and is loved. Such a family is, again, the basis of a stable society, whose members not only feel secure, thanks to a clear recognition of their respective stations and fixed duties, but also derive satisfaction from the assurance of the continuity of generations. Such security is a man's sure anchorage in the turbulent stream of time. A stable society affords its God-fearing, intelligent, and industrious members all the facilities for the enjoyment of their legitimate pleasures.

But earthly happiness terminates with death. Then men long for a happiness more enduring and refined, in the celestial world, which is thus described in the Vedas in the prayer of a dying man:

> The kingdom of inexhaustible light
> Whence is derived the radiance of the sun,
> To this Kingdom transport me,
> Eternal, undying....
> Where there is longing and consummation of longing,
> Where the other side of the sun is seen,
> Where is refreshment and satiety,
> There suffer me to dwell immortal.[1]

To such a heaven fortunate souls repair after death to enjoy the fruits of their worship and meritorious actions. They become gods and lead a long life, beyond anything known to earthly mortals. Then they return to this world and so go through repeated births and deaths.

The highest among the heavenly planes is *Brahmaloka,* the abode of Brahma or the Creator God. This is a place of intensely spiritual atmosphere, whose inhabitants live, free from disease, old age, and death, enjoying uninterrupted bliss in the companionship of the Deity. They never return to the earth for rebirth. The attainment of *Brahmaloka* is the highest aspiration of the worshiper of the Personal God. In *Brahmaloka* the Ultimate Reality reveals itself to a Christian as the Father-in heaven, to a Moslem as Allah, to a Jew as Jehovah, and to the worshipper of Vishnu as Vishnu. The dwellers of this heaven, free from all material desires, retain their individuality, without any earthly stain, for the enjoyment of God's love. They regard themselves as parts of the Deity.

The *Taittirīya Upaniṣad* gives a graphic description of the bliss of *Brahmaloka,* comparing it to the happiness of earth and other celestial planes. The full measure of human bliss, the *Upanishad* says, is enjoyed by "a young man — a noble young man — versed in the Vedas, the best of the rulers, firm in body and strong, and the master of the whole world full of wealth."[2] (The same bliss increases a hundredfold as one ascends from one heaven to another, as a result of the gradual elimination of selfishness, and finds its culmination in *Brahmaloka.* The hierarchy among the gods or other dwellers in the heavens is determined by the differences in the density of the veil of *māyā* or ignorance that no embodied individual can completely get rid of. Brahma too is associated with *māyā,* though a *māyā* extremely fine, which he, furthermore, keeps under his control. Beyond *Brahmaloka* is the supreme bliss of *Brahman* or the Pure Spirit, as experienced by an illumined person who has realized his total identity with It. The bliss of *Brahman* is absolute and does not admit of any higher or lower degree. All phenomenal beings, subject to *māyā,* from man upward to *Brahma,* experience only a reflection of that bliss, depending upon the measure of purity, non-attachment, and meritorious action of each individual.

Brahmaloka too, is a part of the created universe, and comes to an end at the time of cosmic dissolution, when its dwellers merge in *Brahman* and attain to liberation. But an earnest non-dualist longs for liberation through Self-knowledge in this very life. Either through the actual experiences of previous births or through knowledge based upon discrimination, he has realized the transitory value of all enjoyments through various bodies — ranging from a blade of grass to Brahma, or the Creator God — and has no desire to repeat any of them. Thus, in his "desirelessness", he directly realizes his oneness with *Brahman*.

Now, Nachiketa was not satisfied even with the happiness of *Brahmaloka* and he asked for the third boon, Self-knowledge, which releases one from repeated births and deaths. Thus the story leads to the discussion of *Brahman*.

Nachiketa said to Yama: "There is this doubt about a man when he is dead: some say that he exists, others that he does not. This I should like to know, taught by you. This is the third of my boons." Evidently he realized that there was some indestructible element in man, different from body, sense-organs, and the mind, which the scriptures call *Ātman* or Self, and that through Self-knowledge one attains immortality, and the highest good. But one cannot acquire the true knowledge of Self without cultivating non-attachment from all material objects and desires.

Fitness for Self-knowledge

Yama undertook to test Nachiketa's fitness for Self-knowledge. First, he told him about its inscrutability; even the gods were not quite clear about the matter. He advised Nachiketa to give up the pursuit of a will-o-the-wisp. But the latter remained unshaken in his determination. Then Yama tempted him with various worldly enjoyments, sons and grandsons who would live a hundred years, elephants, horses, cattle, a long life, and lordship over the world. If Nachiketa wanted heavenly maidens with chariots and musical instruments, and other pleasures not easily obtainable by men, they, too, would be his for the mere asking. But nothing could deflect Nachiketa from his goal. As unperturbed as the depth of the ocean, he said to Yama: "But, O Death, these endure only till tomorrow. Furthermore they exhaust the vigor of all the sense organs. Even the longest life (in the universe) is short indeed. Keep your horses, dancers, and songs for yourself. Tell me, O Death, of that Great Hereafter about which a man has his doubts." He surely would not choose any other boon but the one so wrapped in mystery.

Yama had offered Nachiketa all that the world most prizes as most pleasant, but the latter desired only the good. Impressed by Nachiketa's sincerity and earnestness, the King of Death then proceeded to explain the meaning of the pleasant and the good, and the conflicting ends to which they lead. They both exist in the world and are within the reach of man. The wise choose the good, and the fools, the pleasant. Though man in general wants to enjoy both the pleasant and the good at the same time, the two are really wide apart, and as exclusive of each other as darkness and light. One is associated with ignorance and the other with knowledge. Seekers of the pleasant, dwelling in ignorance, are victims of many desires and are entangled in the world. Regarding themselves as clever and wise they lead other ignorant men to sorrow and suffering, like the blind leading the blind, only to be born again in this death-fraught world. The good is never known to those who are negligent, devoid of discrimination, or those who live under the spell of wealth. Victims of greed and avarice, such deluded beings believe that the body and the physical world alone are real.

The knowledge of *Ātman* alone, Yama taught Nachiketa, is the bestower of good.

The nature of *Ātman* is extremely difficult to grasp, he explained, and cannot be known by reasoning, however subtle. Many have not even heard of It, and many who have heard do not comprehend It. *Ātman* is sometimes identified with the body, and sometimes with the mind, and thus diversely regarded by those who try to understand It by reason. The true seeker of *Ātman*, as a result of righteous action of the past, gradually develops non-attachment to material objects and feels a genuine longing for Self-knowledge. He is taught by an illumined teacher who, free from the illusion of duality, has realized the nature of Self, and is free from doubt, since it is the very nature of Self-knowledge to dispel all doubts. Vain is the effort to understand *Ātman* by mere discursive reasoning, which associates It with various notions of the impure mind. The mind cannot be pure unless it has renounced all attachment to material objects on earth or in heavenly worlds, including *Brahmaloka*. Yama highly praised the total dispassion of Nachiketa, who rejected even *Brahmaloka*, where one experiences the culmination of material happiness.

The Nature of Ātman

Now he expounded to Nachiketa the nature of *Ātman* and the discipline for Its realization. *Ātman*, effulgent and self-existent, is the foundation of the universe. It dwells in the body and lies hidden in the intellect. It must be separated from the body, sense organs, and the mind, and concentrated upon to the exclusion of all other thoughts. Nachiketa's desire for Self-knowledge was intense. He implored Yama to describe It more fully because *Ātman* is unlike anything in creation — untouched by righteousness and unrighteousness, time, space, and causation.

Yama said that It is to be meditated upon through the mystic word *Om*, which is also the symbol of *Brahman*. Knowledge of the identity of *Brahman* and *Ātman* is the ultimate goal of the Vedic wisdom, desiring which an aspirant leads a life of austerities, and practices self-control and chastity. *Om* is the symbol for both the Creator God and the attributeless Absolute. By meditating on *Om* one attains to both *Brahmaloka* and finally the pure Spirit.

Continuing the explanation of *Ātman*, Yama said: "The knowing Self is not born; it does not die. It has not sprung from anything, nothing has sprung from It. Birthless, eternal, everlasting, and ancient, It is not killed when the body is killed." Only those who identify *Ātman* with the body speak of killing it or being killed by it. "If the killer thinks he kills and if the killed man thinks he is killed, neither of these apprehends aright. The Self kills not, nor is It killed. *Ātman*, smaller than the small, greater than the great, is hidden in the hearts of all living creatures. A man who is free from desires beholds the majesty of the Self through tranquility of the senses, and the mind and becomes free from grief." The inmost essence of all things, both great and small, *Ātman* is one without a second, though It appears as many because the ignorant identify It with various material forms. Its unique greatness consists in the fact that it neither expands nor contracts by Its seeming association with tangible objects. It does not become holy through a man's good actions nor sinful through his evil actions, because It is never truly attached. But evil actions create a veil concealing Its natural purity and effulgence, and good actions remove the veil. Illumined persons realize clearly that *Ātman*, though incorporeal, dwells in impermanent bodies and is not overcome by the grief and sorrows of life.

Though inscrutable, *Ātman* is not altogether unknown and unknowable. True, It cannot be known through the study of the scriptures or the power of intellect; these can only suggest the possibility of Its existence. For Its direct realization both self-effort and divine grace are necessary. Self-effort removes obstacles and creates the condition for the spontaneous revelation of *Ātman*. When the wind blows away the cloud that hides the sun, then the refulgent orb becomes manifest. An aspirant, entangled in the world, after making much effort through scriptural study, reasoning, and meditation, realizes his inadequacy because these disciplines do not altogether free him from ego.

As long as he retains even the slightest trace of ego, he does not realize *Ātman*. He at last totally surrenders himself to God and solicits His grace. Grace is the bestower of liberation, but self-effort is necessary. Unless the seeker, through actual experience, is convinced of the futility of self-effort, he cannot practice self-surrender and receive divine grace. The real Self is always present behind man's thoughts, words, and actions. But It is not recognized in the absence of self-effort. He alone, Yama emphasized, who has refrained from evil conduct and practiced self-control, who has gathered his mind from the outside world and does not disturb it even by seeking the fruit of spiritual practices, attains Self-knowledge with the help of a qualified teacher and by God's grace.

Self-knowledge refers to the knowledge of the Higher Self, and self-control to the control of the lower self, without which injunctions for the practice of the spiritual disciplines and the desire for liberation would be meaningless. The individual soul is attached to the body, and is a victim of pleasure and pain, good and evil, hunger and thirst, and other pairs of opposites. Limited in knowledge and power, it is bound by the apparently interminable chain of birth and death and seeks deliverance from it. Toward that end it studies the scriptures, receives instruction from a qualified teacher, and practices various spiritual disciplines.

The Supreme Soul, on the other hand, is eternally free, illumined, and pure. Whereas the individual soul experiences the fruit of action, good and bad, the Supreme Soul remains the unattached witness. Both the individual soul and the Supreme Soul dwell in the body and are located in the heart, which is the seat of intellect. The individual soul is a reflection of the Supreme Soul in the mirror of intellect. Inside the heart, according to the Vedic seers, there is an *ākāśa,* a luminous space, infinitely subtler and purer than the outer *ākāśa*, which is described as the *Brahma-puram*, or the abode of *Brahman*. In the deepest meditation the limited intellect of the individual merges in the unlimited consciousness of the Supreme Self. The purpose of spiritual discipline is to enable the individual soul to transcend the limitations created by ignorance and realize its oneness with the Supreme Soul.

The Discipline of Self-Control

Having thus discussed Self-knowledge and the Supreme Soul, Yama next proceeded to an exposition of the discipline of self-control.

The individual soul, he said, is endowed with a physical body, the ten sense-organs — five organs of action and five of perception — the mind (*manas*) which views everything as problematic, the intellect (*buddhi*) which resolves doubts, the *citta* which is the store-house of past impressions, and the I-consciousness (*ahaṁkāra*). These consist of material particles, gross or subtle, and are the instrument of actions and perceptions, which bring experiences to the soul. The universe supplies the field for these experiences. The individual soul, identified with the universe, can perform the action either for the fulfillment of worldly desires or for the attainment of ultimate liberation. A man is free to choose either of these courses: he is guided by his desires.

The King of Death likened self-control to the driving of a chariot. The master desires to go to a certain place and orders his chariot. The driver is seated in front controlling the horses by means of reins. If the chariot is well built and the driver knows his way, if the reins are strong, the horses healthy and firmly controlled, and the right roads chosen, then the master will easily reach his destination. If, on the other hand, the chariot is dilapidated, the driver confused about the right path, the reins weak, and the horses unmanageable, then the master cannot reach his goal. Now let us apply this illustration to the spiritual journey. The soul entangled in the world is the master who seeks the goal of liberation. The body is the chariot, the intellect the driver, the mind the reins, the sense organs are the horses, and various objects of the physical world are like the roads helpful or detrimental to the realization of a man's spiritual goal. If the intellect loses its discriminative power and cannot rightly direct the mind, then the senses become uncontrolled like the vicious horses of a charioteer. "If the intellect possesses discrimination and restrains the mind, the senses come under control, like the good horses of a charioteer." A man lacking self-control loses his discrimination, never attains the goal, and "enters into rounds of births." But if, on the other hand, he possesses discrimination and practices self-control, he remains pure and attains the goal from which he cannot again be separated. "A man who has discrimination for his charioteer, and holds the reins of the mind firmly, reaches the end of the road," which is the liberation of the Spirit from the bondage of matter.

The *Kaṭha Upaniṣad* states that a keen intellect, able to discriminate between the good and the pleasant, and a strong power of the mind, which can discard the pleasant and pursue the good, are the two important elements in the discipline to be practiced by aspirants. The torture of the body and the weakening of the sense organs, through irrational austerities, are detrimental to spiritual development. Love of God cannot grow in an arid heart.

What is the goal of man's spiritual journey? Is it a celestial plane far away in space to be reached by following a particular path? The King of Death taught Nachiketa that the goal lies within man himself and is to be realized by the inwardness of the mind. It is man's true essence, which is not seen because of ignorance. It is the *Ātman* or the Self, which is the subtlest element in man — subtler than the sense organs, the mind, the intellect, and the cosmic mind. Beyond the *Ātman* there is nothing. This is the end, the Supreme Goal. The Self should be distinguished from material objects, including the senses and the mind. The aspirant should constantly meditate on its identity with *Brahman* or Pure Spirit.

The Discipline of Meditation

What is the discipline of meditation? Yama described what is called *yoga* to Nachiketa. "The wise should merge his speech in his mind, and his mind in the intellect. Next he merges his intellect in the Cosmic Mind and Cosmic Mind in the tranquil Self." In other words, the aspirant should restrain the activities of the sense organs and direct his attention to the mind. Next he should merge the mind which creates desires and doubts into the intellect which projects the notion of individuality. Then he should merge the intellect into Cosmic Mind where individuality disappears. Finally, the intense urge of the seeker rends the thin veil of the Cosmic Mind and reveals the glories of *Ātman*. Thus a man becomes free from the jaws of death and enjoys peace and blessedness. The *Upanishad* therefore exhorts all: "Arise! Awake! Approach the great (the illumined teacher) and learn. Like the sharp edge of a razor is that path, so the wise say — hard to tread and difficult to cross."

The main obstacle to Self-knowledge is the tendency of the mind to dwell on objects other than the Self. This brooding creates attachment, which in its turn stimulates desire to possess those objects. The frustration of desire is followed by anger, which produces delusion. A deluded person forgets himself, loses the power of discrimination, and ultimately becomes spiritually dead. Why does one dwell on externals, on physical objects? Yama said that the Supreme Lord, who is independent and accountable to none for His actions, "has created the sense organs with outgoing tendencies; therefore a man perceives the outer world and not the inner Self." This is called *māyā*, the cause of creation, natural and beginningless; it is inherent in creation. There would be no physical world without *māyā*. Reason cannot adequately explain it, for the mind itself belongs to *māyā*. But it is within the power of man to turn the senses from the world through discrimination and behold the inner Self with "eyes closed." To the person who has turned his sense organs from the outside world, the immortal nature of *Ātman* is revealed. It is an uphill task, like the turning back of a swift river from its downward course.

Non-discriminating people, identified with the body and attached to desires, are entangled in the meshes of repeated births and deaths. Therefore, the "calm souls," conscious of their true nature, "do not covet any uncertain thing in this world." One cannot escape death through longing for progeny, wealth, or life in heaven — the three main desires cherished by the ignorant.

How does *Ātman*, knowledge of which Nachiketa requested as his third boon, function in the physical body? "It is through *Ātman* that one knows form, taste, smell, sound, touch, and carnal pleasure." There is nothing unknown to *Ātman*. It is Pure Consciousness, the Subject, the unattached Witness. All external objects, including the body, the senses, and the mind, are witnessed by *Ātman*. When a sense organ perceives an object, *Ātman* uses it as the organ of perception. Without the presence of *Ātman* nothing can act. Iron filings move in the presence of a magnet. Under the light of a lamp, various actions are performed. The lamp is the unattached perceiver. *Ātman* does not directly participate in any actions, nor is It affected by their results. "It is through *Ātman* that one perceives all objects in sleep or in the waking state." *Ātman* is the non-attached Witness of the activities in those states and also of their absence in dreamless sleep.

Ātman reflected in the intellect *(buddhi)* and identified with the body, through ignorance, appears as the individual or the embodied soul. When ignorance is destroyed through Self-knowledge, the individual soul realizes its true nature. Thus the illumined person sees himself in all and all in himself. "He does not conceal Himself from others." He becomes natural, spontaneous, and free. As long as a man regards himself as different from others, he is a victim of fear and suspicion and tries to conceal his thoughts and actions. The knower of non-duality is not secretive. He lives and works remembering constantly his identity with all.

Brahman, desirous of creation, projects the universe and the individual souls out of Itself, without any external compulsion, and pervades them as life and consciousness, whether latent or manifest. The *Upanishad* describes created objects as the sparks from a blazing fire or the music produced by a flute. The universe and the individual souls are essentially the same as *Brahman*, as gold ornaments are the same material as gold. The knowledge of the universe and the individual creature will eventually lead to the knowledge of *Brahman*.

Eliminating Ignorance

Emphasizing that there is no real difference between the phenomenal world and *Brahman*, Yama said to Nachiketa: "What is here, the same is there; what is there, the same is here. He goes from death to death who sees any difference here." The perceiver of difference is subject to repeated births and deaths. The apparent difference between objects characterized by names and forms is the result of ignorance. It is only in the mind purified by the practice of spiritual disciplines that the non-dual *Brahman* is revealed.

Brahman is made manifest through meditation on the luminous space in the heart. This space is pure light without a trace of the smoke of worldliness. *Brahman* is always the same, unaffected by past, present, and future. The perceiver of duality pursues different material goals and loses himself in the world. He is like the rainwater that runs down the sides of a steep hill, divides itself into innumerable channels, and ultimately disappears without having served any useful purpose. Conversely, as pure water poured into pure water becomes one with it, so also the individual soul, by nature free, pure, and illumined, merges in *Brahman* and becomes one with It. The realization of this oneness adds nothing new to the Soul and takes nothing away from It. What is really eliminated is ignorance, which never really existed anyway.

As the knowledge of *Ātman* is extremely subtle and profound, Yama explained it to Nachiketa from another standpoint, by comparing the body and the soul to a city and its king. *Ātman* is the king, and the body the city. The city has certain gates: the eleven apertures or doors, namely the two eyes, the two ears, the two nostrils, the mouth, the navel, the organs of generation and evacuation, and lastly, an aperture on the top of the head through which the life-breath of a *yogi* departs at the moment of death. The body is subject to change but the soul remains changeless. As the king is independent of the city, so also is the soul independent of the body. He who meditates on the non-attached nature of the soul rids himself of desire and obtains freedom even before death.

It may be contended that there must be a different *Ātman* in different bodies. For, in the first place, the death of one person does not imply the death of another. Secondly, the fruit of action performed by one is not reaped by another. Thirdly, the activity of one does not make another active, and so on. The non-dualist does not deny the multiplicity of *Ātman* from the relative standpoint. Because of Its association with different limiting adjuncts, *Ātman* appears to assume different names and forms. The non-dual moon creates many reflections in the waves of a lake. But the limiting adjuncts do not belong to *Ātman's* essential nature, just as the reflected moons are not the real moon. They are adventitious, superimposed by *māyā*, which is nothing but ego and desire. The apparent *Ātman* may be many, but the real *Ātman* is one without a second. Though It functions through various phenomenal objects, Its essential non-duality is not affected. Fire, for instance, appears as wood-fire or coal-fire on account of its association with wood or coal, yet the basic nature of fire remains unaltered. Though the body and the mind cannot function without *Ātman*, yet the ugliness or the beauty of the body, the virtue or vice, pleasure or pain of the mind cannot affect *Ātman*. The eyes cannot see without the sun, yet their blemishes cannot contaminate the sun. The notion that the body and mind are superimposed upon *Ātman* is the fault of ignorance.

The same *Ātman* dwells in all. Yama said: "He is the sun dwelling in the bright heaven. He is air moving in the interspaces. He is the fire dwelling on earth. He is the guest dwelling in the house. He dwells in men, in the gods, in truth, in the sky. He is born in the water, in the sacrifice, on the mountain. He is the True and the Great." *Ātman*, being *Brahman*, excludes multiplicity and difference.

Here is evidence indicating the existence of *Ātman* independent of the body. According to Vedantic philosophy, material objects, consisting of parts, serve the purpose of a living being. Thus a house or a vehicle is for the use of a living person; neither serves any purpose of its own. The body, sense organs, and the *prāṇa* or the vital breath are produced by a combination of material particles. Therefore they are directed in their activities by a separate entity whose interest they serve. This entity is the soul, which is, in reality, the non-dual Spirit. The sense organs bring the impressions from the outside world to the embodied soul, as the subjects bring their offerings to the king. The soul enjoys them, gains experience, realizes their impermanent nature, cultivates detachment from the world, and ultimately discovers the true knowledge of *Brahman*. When the soul leaves the body the latter disintegrates like a city when abandoned by the king. At the time of death, the soul is accompanied by the subtle body, consisting of different organs, as the departing king is accompanied by his officers. *Ātman*, which Nachiketa wanted to know, is the spiritual entity in man in whose absence the body cannot live even for an instant. The *Bhagavad Gītā* says: "When the Lord (the soul) acquires a body, and when He leaves it, He takes away these with Him and goes on His way, as the wind carries away the scents from their places. Presiding over the ears and the eyes, the organs of touch, taste, and smell, and also over the mind, He experiences these sense objects. The deluded do not perceive Him when He departs from the body or dwells in it, when He experiences objects or is united with matter, but they who have the eye of wisdom often perceive Him. Those who strive, armed with *yoga*, behold Him dwelling within themselves; but the undisciplined and the thoughtless do not perceive Him, though they strive."

What Happens After Death?

Now Yama directly answers the question as to what happens after death. If the soul leaves the body after a man has attained to knowledge of the soul's identity with *Brahman*, he is not born again. But what about the unillumined persons? "Some *jīva-s* (embodied souls) enter the world to be born again as organic beings, and some go into inorganic matter — according to their work and according to their knowledge." Here the King of Death speaks of the Law of Karma and rebirth as applied to those who die without attaining Self-knowledge. The future of the embodied soul is determined by its past action and knowledge. By good action it becomes good, and by evil action it becomes evil. It can assume any body in the relative world ranging from the body of a god to that of a plant. Desires and attachments at the hour of death determine the future body through which they will be fulfilled. If *sattva* prevails at the time of death, one obtains a god's body; if *rajas*, a human body, and if *tamas*, a sub-human body. But it must be remembered that the real nature of *Ātman* does not change through the process of rebirth, just as It is not altered when, in dream, the soul creates various forms and identifies itself with them. It remains the same pure Spirit, the witness of changes during the rebirth or dream.

Through *avidyā* or nescience, the Spirit appears as manifold. The realization of Its true nature should be the goal of a man's strivings. This knowledge brings him peace. Yama said: "There is one supreme Ruler, the inmost Self of all beings, who makes His one form manifold. Eternal happiness belongs to the wise who perceive Him within themselves — not to others.

There is One who is the eternal Reality among non-eternal objects, the only (real) conscious Entity among (apparently) conscious objects, and who, though non-dual, fulfills the desires of many. Eternal peace belongs to the wise who perceive Him within themselves — not to others." When the light of *Ātman* illumines the heart, the radiance of the sun, the moon, and the lightning pales into insignificance. When *Ātman* shines, everything shines; and by Its light all are lighted.

Continuing his teachings, Yama said that as from the sight of the cotton lying far away from the tree, blown by the wind, one can infer the existence of the cotton tree, so also by investigating the nature of the universe one can infer the existence of *Brahman*, its root and unseen cause. The tree of *saṁsāra*, or the universe, with its unceasing births and deaths, is without beginning or end. But unlike the ordinary tree, the tree of *saṁsāra* grows with its root above, which is *Brahman*. Its branches — which are various heavens or nether worlds or other spheres inhabited by embodied souls — spread downwards into the realm of time, space, and causality. The whole creation arises in *Brahman*, rests in It, and finally disappears into It, as is the case with the waves and the ocean. The universe cannot transcend *Brahman*, as the effect cannot go beyond the cause. Though in itself inert and non-intelligent, it vibrates with life and consciousness, because *Brahman*, which pervades it, is life and consciousness. Under the control of Almighty Spirit everything in the universe performs its function. "From terror of *Brahman*, fire burns; from terror of It, the sun shines; from terror of It, *Indra* (the king of the gods) and *Vayu* (the god of wind), and Death, the fifth, run." The presence of *Brahman* imparts physical and moral order to the creation, which would otherwise be chaotic.

Attaining to Immortality

"*Brahman* must be realized in this very life before the falling asunder of the body." Then alone is a man liberated; otherwise he is embodied again in the physical world. "Whosoever in the world, O *Gargi*, without knowing the Imperishable, offers oblations, performs sacrifices, and practices austerities, even for many thousands of years, finds all such acts but perishable. Whosoever, O *Gargi*, departs from the world without knowing this Imperishable is miserable. But he, O *Gargi*, who departs from this world after knowing the Imperishable is a knower of *Brahman*."

Brahman is clearly experienced in a man's intellect, when purified by self-control and meditation, as is one's reflection in a clean mirror. In other words, Its manifestation is distinct. In order to realize *Brahman* one has to separate It from the senses, the mind, and the external objects of the physical world. It is not experienced by the sense organs, but revealed in the intellect, freed from doubt through constant meditation.

A man acquires "cleansed perception" when the senses and the mind are turned inward. His whole body becomes spiritualized. Through all his thoughts and actions such a person communes with *Brahman*. His "everyday mind" never loses contact with *Brahman*.

But mere intellectual knowledge gathered from books or reasoning is not enough. It is absolutely necessary to practice yoga, which enables one to control the sense organs and purify the mind. A *yogi* must be vigilant, for yoga, if improperly practiced, can be injurious. Unless guided by a qualified teacher, the result of yoga can be lost. The teacher helps in destroying the lingering doubts of the student. He guides the student by gradual stages. The latter is first taught to concentrate on *Brahman* as the Personal God, the Creator, the Preserver and the Destroyer; or on *Ātman* controlling the sense organs and the mind. Gradually he is trained to concentrate on *Brahman* or *Ātman* free from all association with limiting adjuncts. Finally, if the seeker is earnest and wants to go deeper, *Brahman* Itself, as it were, removes the veil of *māyā*, and reveals Its true transcendental form. Both grace and proper conditioning of the mind through personal effort are necessary for this profound mystical experience.

Finally Yama concludes his teaching by telling Nachiketa how, while dwelling in the human body, one can attain to Immortality. Desirelessness is the condition. "When all the desires that dwell in the heart fall away, then the mortal becomes immortal and here attains *Brahman*. When all the ties of the heart are severed here on earth, then the mortal becomes immortal. This much alone is the teaching." If a person knows that he is all and all is he, then "for whose sake and desiring what, should he wear out his body day after day?"

The *Kaṭha Upaniṣad* concludes with the inspiring exhortation: "The *Ātman*, not larger than a thumb, always dwells in the hearts of men. Let a man separate It from his body with steadfastness, as one separates the tender stalk from a blade of grass."

The last verse declares: "Having received this wisdom taught by the King of Death, and the entire process of yoga, Nachiketa became free of impurities and death and attained *Brahman*. Thus it will be also with any other who knows, in this manner, the inmost Self."

Footnote

[1]   *Ṛg Veda*, IX.C X 111,7,10,11
[2]   *Taittirīya Upaniṣad* II.VIII.I.

XI

Reincarnation and Immortality

by Swami Shantananda

[The following article is transcribed from a discourse given at a retreat on February 19, 2000, at Toronto, Canada]

The desire for immortality is inherent in every one of us. To re-discover our birth-less and deathless nature is the ultimate goal of human life. In fact it is our birthright. Immortality is not a state which is attained after death, it can be attained right here and now. It is such a unique possession that we must do whatever it takes to reclaim it. Let me explain this by way of an analogy: Suppose you did not know that your father was wealthy, and it was only after his death that you discovered that there was money in a secret bank account. Once you have made this discovery you will naturally struggle to get it. You may not need it, but you will say, "It is not the money that I am fighting for, but it is my birthright." And you will do whatever it takes to make it your own.

In the same way, Vedanta asserts that immortality is our birthright and the intense struggle to regain it is called spiritual living. Before we can focus on immortality however, we need to look into the topic of reincarnation. This is a popular subject these days, and there are many approaches to the idea of reincarnation or rebirth. The Hindu philosophers offer an explanation acceptable to our intellect as they substantiate the theory of rebirth through the following three aspects: 1) By taking into account the words of the scriptures (*śruti*), 2) developing strong tautological reasoning (*yukti*), and 3) conforming this derived knowledge with our own experiences (*anubhava*).

Validity of the Scriptures

First and foremost the sages declare that the scriptures are not the result of a mere intellect, but they constitute the words of the Lord Himself. This being the case, the scriptures do not suffer from a human defect. No matter how exalted the human intellect is, it is still finite and cannot embrace the entire range of knowledge in this world. No one can in one human life claim that he has seen or known everything. We see this every day in the world of science, where a newly discovered theory replaces an existing old one. But the scriptures, namely the Vedas, are considered beyond human thought. And when the scriptures reveal certain statements about sin and merit, concepts that are closely connected to the topic of reincarnation, the average mind is unable to perceive them, because the concepts belong to the realm of the unseen. This can be explained in the following way: Whenever we perform an action there are two results; one of them is experienced immediately and the other remains veiled. The unseen results are stored in our subconscious and these recorded impressions are called *samskāra-s* or *vāsanā-s*. In modern terminology they are similar to computer programs. Each one of us comes with a 'software bundle' and how we apply this program determines our successes and failures in life. The ability to wield this program judiciously is called free will (*puruṣārtha*).

The scriptures are full of statements that validate the cycle of life and death enabling us to make wise choices in our earthly sojourn. For instance, in the *Kaṭhopaniṣad* a young boy Nachiketa enters into a dialogue with the King of Death himself to find answers to his questions about life and death. [*Ref: Ch. X,*

Is Death the End? by Swami Nikhilananda, p. 92.] There are also many references in the *Bhagavad Gītā*. "Even as a person casts off worn-out clothes and puts on others that are new, so the embodied Self casts off worn-out bodies and enters into others that are new." (2:22) So these are the statements where *śruti* and *smṛti* both talk of existence of the soul after death. But is it valid logically?

Validity of Logic

The concept of reincarnation revealed to us in our scriptures can be explained by logic or yukti. Today it is easy for us to explain the concept of all-pervasiveness because of the current scientific understanding of infinity. If we say that this birth is a fresh start and there was no past, would it not be a contradiction? We all know that every action has an equal and opposite reaction. We know from our own experiences in life that if we perform an action we receive a result. The result is immaterial, but a result will not come to us without a preceding action. Therefore, if we say that this life is an effect without a cause, it is illogical, as there must be a past before the present. Even when a person wins a lottery it is not an accident; he must have worked for it in some previous life. We say that he was lucky only because our intellect is unable to explain the cause. But that does not mean there was no cause to begin with.

Having come to this world we have many ambitions to fulfill, and we are not always able to complete each and every one of them. Let us say that for some reason we have to leave a project unfinished. What happens to the effort that has so far been poured into the project? According to the Law of Nature if we have worked for something (action) we must get the result (reaction). The person putting in the effort and the person receiving the result have to be the same; they cannot be two different individuals. Similarly, if we say that this present life is an accident or a fresh start, it then amounts to saying that we are getting the result without having earned it. Furthermore, if we say that death is a full stop to life, then the cause is there (means worked for it) but the effect (result) is not received. Therefore, the standpoint of one life seems illogical any way we look at it. We have done something that did not produce a result, or we get a result without first doing anything for it. Both are contrary to logic or *yukti* as we do not see this demonstrated in our daily life.

Validity of Experience

Although a theory can be proven to be true logically, it is not valid unless it conforms to our own experience (anubhava). Let us see how the theory of reincarnation conforms to our own experience first from the standpoint of diversity:

Why are we all different? If the Lord created everyone out of His own Self, as maintained by Hindu scriptures, then all of us should be the same. However, if you ask ten children to speak on the same topic, they will all say something different, based on their past experiences. Some are child prodigies and some juvenile delinquents. Similarly, among adults, we will find men and women of great accomplishment, and also those who have experienced only failure in their lives. Some people have a tendency to be dishonest, others are brilliant and talented, and some are born with physical or mental handicaps. The very fact that these differences exist means that there must have been a different past. These differences are commonly seen in birth and social status on the physical, emotional, and mental levels.

Each of us is unique, not only physically, but also in our mental makeup and intellectual thinking. Some of us are able to think independently and some are not. Our children also come with their own tendencies and because of our delusion (*moha*) we think that we can control and shape them. We can only provide certain circumstances and create a healthy atmosphere for them to grow in. The very fact that we see differences means that there must be a past. Without a past we cannot explain the differences logically.

There are also different ways in which we express love. Suppose you are waiting at a railway platform and someone slaps you on your back, you get angry but the moment you realize it is your friend, the emotion of anger changes to love. Emotions too, are expressed in different ways when directed toward different objects and we can experience the changes in our own mind. If I ask you, "Do you love your wife more than your mother?" How will you answer? The emotion of love that is directed towards your wife is totally different from the one directed towards your mother.

Thus, we have earned every one of our experiences; there are no accidents in life. We say it is an accident because we do not know the cause. Once we recognize the cause it becomes an incident, it is an incident that happened in time and space. We worked hard even for the suffering that we experience in life. Therefore we should take full responsibility for all that happens in life and not blame anyone else. According to the Law of Karma we are all architects of our own fate. But how are sin and merit (*pāpa* and *puṇya*) and the Law of Karma interconnected?

The Many Aspects of Sin and Merit

The entire theory of karma and of sin and merit is rather fascinating and needs to be thoroughly understood. Usually when we perform an action we first think about it. This then becomes a voluntary, deliberate action that can either be meritorious or sinful. We can tell which kind it is by the reaction we experience after it is performed. If we touch a live wire, the reaction will be immediate. Similarly, after performing an action, if our intellect (*buddhi*) continuously condemns us and we feel miserable then we know that it is a sinful action. In Gurudev's (Swami Chinmayananda) words, "We are not punished for the sin, but by the sin." When, on the other hand, we perform a righteous act the result will immediately invoke joy within us.

Due to our merits (*punya-s*) we gain happiness in life. Happiness being our essential nature, we want to stay happy. Naturally then when unhappiness is experienced due to sins, we want to escape from it. Why does sin create unhappiness within us? And what is sin? The psychological conflict that is created between the ideal and the real is called sin. Most of us have ideals and goals, but because of our weaknesses we are not able to raise ourselves up to those ideals. When the mind is able to live up to an ideal without conflict, the mind is in a meritorious state.

When our actions, either sinful or meritorious, are repeated they tend to become habits, which are carried with us through many lives. During this great pilgrimage of life, when we are able to understand the cycle of action and reaction, only then can we begin to change our binding habits, which we ourselves have created. In fact, man's eternal struggle is to re-program and reduce the *samskāra-s* or *vāsanā-s* that we have carried with us all the way from the past to the present life. This necessitates that we acquire a correct vision of life, which is provided by our scriptures.

A devotee once asked: "I am confused about sin, my intellect tells me that some of my actions are bad, but I still continue to perform them?" The answer is, "Continue, do not stop. If your mind regrets an action, yet the next moment you do the same thing, don't stop immediately. For example, if you are driving on the freeway and miss your exit, you cannot stop suddenly, as this would cause an accident. The only way is to make a U-turn cautiously at the next exit, then turn around again in the direction you were headed earlier. It is the same for a person who commits sins continuously. Slow down, prepare the mind and then take the turn."

This requires that we should be very aware of our thoughts and actions, because what our future holds will depend on how we live right now. It is true that the past has influenced the way we think and act in the present moment, but we can still navigate it in the right direction if we are well informed. This navigational technique is given in the *Bhagavad Gītā*. It is only after Lord Krishna imparts this great knowledge that Arjuna is able to face all the challenges in life. At the beginning of the Mahabharata war, Arjuna was confused because his mind was overwhelmed with emotion. In the same way, when we are too sentimental we tend to justify and rationalize our wrong actions. But once we realize our mistake and feel genuine remorse we begin to change, even if we are the worst sinners.

We need to know that the entire problem is within ourselves. Our mind is a battlefield, a *Kurukṣetra,* and there is always a struggle for righteous living, dharma. It is only by living a *dhārmika* way of life that we feel content and happy, anything contrary we pay for in terms of sorrow and agitation. How can we correct it? By being aware of our thoughts. We should be able to recognize any thought that rises in our mind, and know the consequences of thinking that particular thought. If we are not alert enough, however, our mind will continue to collect thoughts, and when we are in our meditation room we will naturally be thinking of the many things that we have stored in the mind.

Finally, it is the duty of the parents to understand this vision for living a *dhārmika* life, and to teach their children the difference between right and wrong. We may sometimes feel that in doing so we are conditioning our children's minds and preventing them from discovering life on their own. But by not teaching our children we are abdicating our parental duty. They may not accept them while they are young, but once we have planted the right seeds they will eventually see the merit of these teachings when faced with situations brought about by life's experiences. Since we have the choice to make or mar ourselves why not use this gift of God and aim for the highest, which is the state of Immortality?

Immortality: Our Birthright

How do we end the cycle of birth and death? If we perform a particular action the result is inevitable. Similarly, we perform millions of actions but we will not be able to get the result from every action in this very life. Thus we are not only born with inherent tendencies (*vāsanā-s*) but while living and interacting with others we also add to them. We have to take many lives because we have to exhaust so many different desires. Hence the cycle of birth and death is endless. At the same time we want to get out of the cycle, but while trying to do so we perform actions that bind us more. It is just like being in quicksand. The more we struggle to get out of the quicksand, the more we become caught. Sinful actions make the veil of ignorance thicker, and virtuous actions makes it thinner. Once our *vāsanā-s* start thinning out we will reach a point where quietude comes to us automatically, and we will stop struggling.

We find that all the desires that we have in this world fall under three categories: (1) we all want to live a day more, (2) we want to know everything, and (3) we want to be happy permanently.

We all want to live forever. We know that physically this is not possible; therefore we desire progeny, as having children will insure us that our name will be carried on. So too, there are the artisans who want to create lasting works of beauty in the form of music, art or sculpture, or the philanthropists who desire to leave their names on monuments and institutions. Life is sweet; therefore, the mind gets attached to the physical body even if it is useless. In the Hindu *Purāna-s*, there is a story of a young devotee, Prahlad. Through a boon granted by the Lord, Prahlad wished to take his family and friends to heaven with him, but they all made excuses for living one more day. They declined to go with Prahlad because of their physical attachment to this life and this body. This very attachment to our physical entity tells us that we want to live eternally.

Besides wanting to live eternally we also want to know everything. Why do we read newspapers and watch the news? It is not that we are going to change the world. Our knowing or not knowing does not make much difference, but still we are always curious. The very fact that we are not able to contend with ignorance shows that our nature is to gain infinite knowledge, due to which we are able to use our intellect effectively.

In addition to our desire for eternity and infinite knowledge, we also crave everlasting happiness. In time and space there is limitation and any limitation, whether it is physical, emotional, or intellectual produces sorrow. This veils the happiness (*ānanda*) which is our true nature. Vedanta asserts that we are eternal, infinite, and all-knowing. Once we know that we are not limited, our intellect is transcended, and we experience that blissful state.

In the midst of all action, reaction, birth and death why do we crave for permanence and peace, for immortality and bliss? The very fact that we are not able to accept these changes shows that we have an eye for "changelessness." That we are unable to acknowledge any limitation tells us that we are intrinsically free, but do not recognize it. Due to this inherent longing for permanence and freedom we are unable to settle for small things. In life once we have tasted the best we do not want to settle for anything less. The same is true for our true nature; it is the best. That is why we are not able to accept anything less, hence the struggle.

We want *Sat-cit-ānanda*. *Sat* means everlasting existence. *Cit* means awareness and true knowledge. That knowledge which makes us conscious of what is happening in our bodies and thoughts is called "awareness." *Ānanda* indicates the happiness that we experience when all limitations are removed. When we are happy we do not complain. This is because happiness is our natural state.

With the same intensity with which we fight for our rights

we should strive to reclaim our birthright, which is immortality. If that intensity is felt, liberation is around the corner. Until that suffocating intensity is felt, however, we have to learn from teachers and scriptures. There is a story of a student, a spiritual aspirant, who approached a teacher and asked him to please give liberation. The teacher took him to a lake and held his head under water. The teacher said, " When you feel that intensity for gaining liberation as you did trying to get your head above the water for air, you will get it!" It has to become a number one priority. How then do we seek that blessed state?

First, the mind has to be steadied through certain disciplines. A disciplined mind is a steady mind, a mind devoid of worldly desires. Rise to that particular point where God alone is important, nothing else. The person for whom the Lord alone is the highest achievement is referred to as *Pārtha*, the name by which Lord Krishna addressed Arjuna. This should be our only goal.

Thinking that we are the body, mind, and intellect we have become bound in the cycle of life and death. And this erroneous notion has been brought about by ego, *ahaṁkāra*. Because of ego we give priority to immediate benefits, and we have become slaves to our body, mind, and intellect. Immediate sense gratification has created a cocoon around us. To break out of this shell is to recognize and own up to our true nature, which we call *mukti* or *mokṣa*. This is liberation and freedom with reference to body, mind, and intellect. A person who is self-realized, a *jīvan mukta puruṣa*, is freed from all these limitations. For an onlooker he may be functioning through the body like any one else. And we may think that he is conditioned, but in his own Self he is free and above it all. *Jīvanmukti* is the state of being liberated while living. And it is possible to achieve it in this very life!

Go within yourself, introspect and discover that the Lord is right there, waiting for you to come to Him. Once you are convinced you will begin to practice and make a commitment. Begin with small steps, and don't think a little effort is meaningless. Concentrate and repeat the name of the Lord for ten minutes every day and try to focus on the meaning of the words. Be sincere. Even if your mind is thinking idly let it think about all the stories of the Lord. These small steps will slowly lead to a change. Practice meditation and seek the company of saintly people, and some teacher will come to guide you. You don't have to search for him. The guru will come to you, that is nature's rule. Wherever you are, improve and purify yourself, dedicate all your actions to the Lord, and He Himself will send the guru to guide and help you and end the cycle of birth and death.

XII

The Great Awakening

by Eknath Easwaran

As we enter the second half of life, if we are sensitive, we will begin to suspect that we cannot put our trust in any changing relationship based on physical attraction, or even in a relationship based on sympathy of mind or intellect. All these shift and alter with the passage of time. The only relationship that is permanent is the relationship between the Self in you and the same Self in others; the spiritual relationship in which we forget ourselves in living for the welfare of all. As the Upanishads say, "A wife loves her husband not for his own sake, but because the Self lives in him. A husband loves his wife not for her own sake, but because the Self lives in her. Children are loved not for their own sake, but because the Self lives in them. All creatures are loved not for their own sake, but because the Self lives in them."

In personal relationships we should try to observe the kind of restraint Epictetus recommends. "Remember, to behave in life as you would behave at a banquet. When something is being passed around, as it comes to you, stretch out your hand and take a portion of it politely. When it passes on, do not try to hold on to it; when it has not yet come to you, do not reach out for it with your desire but wait until it presents itself. So act toward children, toward spouse, toward office, toward wealth."

Don't try to cling to people and hold them to you: everything changes, and if you try to arrest relationships and hold on to others, making them conform to your own needs, the light of love is extinguished very soon. This is the real meaning of detachment. It's not running away from life, but having no particular, private, personal attachments: not the absence of love but the fullness of love for all.

The word *detachment* has a cold sound in English, but it is only when we have this kind of perfect spiritual detachment that our compassion extends to every creature. We will see in the death of any creature the fate of us all. "Never send to know for whom the bell tolls; it tolls for thee," as John Donne said. Whenever any creature or any person dies, we lose a part of ourselves.

The key to this universal compassion is given in the *Bhagavad Gītā*: "beyond the reach of 'I and mine.'" If you want to ascend the highest peak that a human being can climb, this is one of the most agonizing qualifications: no sense of "mine" at all, neither with things nor with people. And as if that weren't enough, the *Gītā* adds "not a trace of *ahaṁkāra*." *Ahaṁkāra* is one of those simple yet profound Sanskrit words that is impossible to translate into English. Made up of two smaller words, *ahaṁ*, "I," and *kāra*, "maker," it implies egotism and self-will: in general, too great a measure of self-regard and too great a following after our own passions and inclinations. *Saṁnyāsa*, perfect detachment, ultimately means detachment from our own selfish impulses and inclinations.

The remedy for *ahaṁkāra*, in the Buddha's language, is *nirvāṇa*, from *nir*, "out," and *vāṇa*, "to blow." You keep blowing for years and years and one day the fire of selfishness goes out. You don't snuff it out in one day; you have to keep blowing away, in meditation and then during the day, especially in your relationships. This world is a blacksmith's shop, with fires all around, where we return good will for ill will and love for hatred, work harmoniously with others, and put other people's welfare before our own. All these are for putting out the fire of selfishness, which brings a deep sense of wellness to body and mind alike.

To have perfect detachment, the *Gītā* says, we have to rise above not only "I and mine," but also pleasure and pain. This is precise, universal advice. Whether you live in America or in Asia, in a palace or in a hovel, you cannot escape the duality of pleasure and pain that is woven into the very fabric of life. A permanent state of security can never come to any person who is dependent upon external circumstances and satisfactions, for these all have a definite beginning and a finite end. No lasting joy, no lasting security can be ours if we pursue finite things, things that pass away.

But it takes a long time for most of us to learn that pleasure is not permanent. Most people get frustrated because unconsciously this is what all of us are trying to do: isolate ourselves in a pain-free world. That is the desire behind great many technological advances, particularly where drugs are concerned. I am not opposed to painkillers in the hands of a wise physician, but I know too that whatever we do, pain is an integral part of life.

Hostility, too, is an unavoidable part of life. Even if you have ninety-nine persons cheering you, there will always be a hundredth to slander you. That is the nature of life, and to deal with it, we have to learn not to be always on the outlook for appreciation and applause. If people say, "Oh, there is nobody like you," don't get elated. Don't pick up your telephone and call your friends and tell them all the nice things that are being said about you. That's why so many people sink into depression when fortune seems to frown. During reversals of fortune, which will come to all of us, we can maintain our equanimity and tranquility. We do not need any external support because we are complete in ourselves.

Beyond Change and Death

In our ancient Hindu tradition, we say that within every human being there are two forces deep in consciousness. One is the force of infatuation: selfish attachments, delusion, compulsion, hostility, and violence. It is from these that the death-force draws its power. There is infatuation for money, infatuation for pleasure, infatuation for prestige, and the worst, infatuation for power. Jesus warned us of this force when he said, "All they who take the sword shall perish by the sword." The violent force of selfishness drives us toward death, but when we renounce violence and hostility, we go beyond death in this very life.

The sages of both East and West say that detachment and selflessness are a second force, which takes us over death into eternal life. If you can renounce all that is selfish and petty, you will attain the supreme state in which you know you are neither your body nor your mind, but the one Self, utterly beyond change and death.

In my ancestral family, at least when I was growing up, people who were approaching the evening of life made preparations for the great journey. This is the glory of Buddhism and Hinduism: people know that the boat is coming, and they know that they have to put their house in order and prepare to leave their luggage behind. When the time comes, they are prepared. And then a quite extraordinary thing happens: for them Death is no longer a frightening ogre; Death is a doorman. When the time comes, he opens the door and says, "After you!"

> From the unreal, lead me to the real,
> From darkness, lead me to light.
> From death, lead me to immortality.

This sublime prayer for immortality has been repeated in India for thousands of years, and it is as meaningful today as it was millennia ago. Living for pleasure is living in an unreal world, a dark world. The satisfaction that wealth and pleasure can give is as transient as a dream. Living for others — for our family, our community, our country, the whole world — is living in light.

This body of mine is not me but the car I drive. I rent it here; I leave it there. I rent it for a selfless purpose, and after many decades, when it is no longer functioning well, I will leave it....quietly, with no fuss and no regrets.

"Once we attain that abiding joy beyond the senses," the *Bhagavad Gītā* says, "there is nothing more to be desired. We can no longer be shaken even by the heaviest burden of sorrow." When you have received this gift, what more can the world give you? What temptations can the world hold?

Without Self-realization, every satisfaction, every pleasure, every reward will be taken from us sooner or later by death. This is not a morbid reflection. It enriches life, gives it meaning, keeps us aware that every moment is precious. The sooner we begin to wake ourselves up, the better, for there is far to go. But at any age, the best time is now, because Death is walking close beside us.

Any day death can claim any one of us. But if you can wake yourself up, as the Buddha did, you live in freedom everywhere, in this world and the next. Terms like heaven and hell become pointless. Wherever you go is home, and whatever you do will bear good fruit. It doesn't matter when or where. You lose all curiosity about where you are going in your next life. Wherever you go, your life will flower and bear fruit for all.

Just because this body is shed, my life is not at an end. I know that there is a presence inside, a divine resident who will endure. Even after I have shed my physical body, all the love in my heart — which is not physical, not limited by time and space — will continue, and I will come back in a new body to be re-united with those I have loved and who have loved me — over and over again. People who love deeply, who help greatly, will be together again. This realization removes all fear of death from our hearts and gives us not only courage but understanding in the face of death.

In the Buddhist ideal, the *bodhisattva* is one who takes a vow to be reborn again and again to help relieve the suffering of others. You have reached the end of sorrow, yet you are free to say, "That green earth I lived on has become polluted. I can't just stay here and bask in bliss; I have to go back and do whatever I can to help. War is still stalking the earth, and I don't want even one young person to suffer. Let me go back and help to bring people together in harmony."

Your next life is not dependent upon a throw of the dice. It is dependent entirely on you. As you live today, so will your life be tomorrow. No outsider dictates it. As you live in this life, so will your life be next time; no fate ordains it for you. Instead of being afraid of death and what comes after, you can almost look forward to it just as you look forward to a new day, by preparing for your next life here and now. This is the joy of the Buddha's message: take your life in your hands, learn to practice meditation, change selfish modes of thinking into selfless, make your mind secure where it is insecure, extend your love to embrace all life, and then give and give and give.

About the Authors

Swami Abhedananda

Swami Abhedananda, born on October 2, 1866, was one of the direct disciples of Ramakrishna Paramahansa and the spiritual brother of Swami Vivekananda. His life was intimately bound up with the Vedanta movement in the West. From 1897-1921 he lectured all over North America and Europe. He was appreciated for his profound scholarship, intellectual brilliance, oratorical talents, and noble character. After returning to India in 1921 he established centers at Calcutta and Darjeeling. He attained *mahasamadhi* on September 8, 1939.

Christopher M. Bache

Christopher M. Bache has degrees from the University of Notre Dame, Cambridge University, and Brown University, and teaches in the Department of Philosophy and Religious Studies at Youngstown State University. He has written articles for *Dialectica* and *The Journal for the Scientific Study of Religion*, and has received YSU's Distinguished Professor Award for teaching and research. He lives in Poland, Ohio.

Carus, Paul

Paul Carus was editor of the Open Court Publishing Company from 1887 to his death in 1919. As editor of two journals *The Open Court* and *The Monist*, and with the publication of hundreds of books, many written by him, he was a pioneer in introducing the Orient to the West.

Swami Chinmayananda

Swami Chinmayananda, the founder of Chinmaya Mission, was a sage and visionary. He toured the globe tirelessly giving discourses and writing commentaries on the scriptural knowledge of Vedanta, until he left his bodily form in 1993. (See write-up at the end of this book.)

Easwaran, Eknath

Eknath Easwaran was a writer and a professor of English literature in India when he came to the U. S. as a Fulbright scholar. He was the founder and director of the Blue Mountain Center of Meditation in Berkeley. He taught meditation and allied skills to those who wanted to lead active and spiritually fulfilling lives. He wrote twenty-six books that are translated into eighteen languages. Sri Easwaran passed away on October 26, 1999.

Kornfield, Jack

Jack Kornfield was trained as a Buddhist monk in Thailand, Burma, and India and has taught meditation worldwide since 1974. He is one of the key teachers to introduce Theravada Buddhist practice to the West. For many years his work has focused on integrating and bringing alive the great Eastern spiritual teachings in an accessible way for Western students and Western society. He holds a Ph.D. in clinical psychology and is the founding teacher of the Insight Meditation Society.

Swami Nikhilananda

Swami Nikhilananda, a direct disciple of Holy Mother Sri Sarada Devi, was born in a small Indian village in 1895 and was ordained a monk of the Ramakrishna Order in 1924. After spending several years in the Himalayan monastery he was sent to America in 1931. He founded the Ramakrishna-Vivekananda Center of New York in 1933 and was its spiritual leader until his passing away in 1973. Swami Nikhilananda was a gifted writer, and his biggest contribution has been the translation of *The Gospel of Sri Ramakrishna* from Bengali to English.

Swami Shantananda

Swami Shantananda is head of the Chinmaya Mission Tri-State Center that serves the New York, Pennsylvania, New Jersey, and Delaware areas. He was the head of Chinmaya Mission at Hong Kong and Taiwan before assuming his leadership role in the U.S. A disciple of Swami Chinmayananda, he had the rare privilege of traveling with his guru as his secretary. Swamiji is a gifted speaker and travels extensively giving discourses on Indian scriptures and their practical applications in daily life.

Weiss, Brian L.

Brian L. Weiss, M.D. a psychiatrist, lives and practices in Miami, Florida. He is a graduate of Columbia University and Yale Medical School, and is the former Chairman of Psychiatry at the Mount Sinai Medical Center in Miami, Florida.

Swami Yatiswarananda

Swami Yatiswarananda (1889-1966), a former Vice-President of the Ramakrishna Math and Ramakrishna Mission, was a well-known spiritual figure in the Neo-Vedanta movement. He spent several years spreading Vedanta in Europe and the U.S.A. His *Meditation and Spiritual Life* has been acclaimed as a spiritual classic.

Swami Vivekananda

Swami Vivekananda was the foremost disciple of Ramakrishna Paramahansa. He was the founder of the Ramakrishna Mission. He became famous in the West through his address at the Parliament of Religions in Chicago in 1893 that helped focus the world's attention on the Vedantic teachings.

Pronunciation of Sanskrit Letters

a	(b*u*t)	k	(*s*kate)	t	⌠*th*ink or	ś	(*sh*ove)
ā	(f*a*ther)	kh	(*K*ate)	th	⌡*th*ird	ṣ	(bu*sh*el)
i	(*i*t)	g	(*g*ate)	d	⌠*th*is or	s	(*s*o)
ī	(b*ee*t)	gh	(*g*awk)	dh	⌡*th*ere	h	(*h*um)
u	(s*u*ture)	ṅ	(*s*ing)	n	(*n*umb)	ṁ	(nasaliza-
ū	(p*oo*l)	c	(*ch*unk)	p	(*s*pin)		tion of
ṛ	(*r*ig)	ch	(mat*ch*)	ph	(loo*ph*ole)		preceding
ṝ	(*rrr*ig)	j	(*J*ohn)	b	(bu*n*)		vowel)
ḷ	⌠no	jh	(*j*am)	bh	(ru*b*)	ḥ	(aspira-
	⎪ English	ñ	(bu*n*ch)	m	(*m*uch)		tion of
	⎨ equiva-	ṭ	(*t*ell)	y	(*y*oung)		preceding
	⎩ lent	ṭh	(*t*ime)	r	(d*r*ama)		vowel)
e	(pl*ay*)	ḍ	(*d*uck)	l	(*l*uck)		
ai	(h*i*gh)	ḍh	(*d*umb)	v	(*w*ile/*v*ile)		
o	(t*o*e)	ṇ	(u*n*der)				
au	(c*o*w)						

MANANAM BACK ISSUES
(continued from page ii)

The Razor's Edge
Harmony and Beauty
The Question of Freedom
The Pursuit of Happiness
On the Path
Beyond Sorrow
Self-Discovery
The Mystery of Creation
Vedanta in Action
Solitude
The Choice isYours

Other Chinmaya Publication Series:

THE *Self-Discovery* SERIES

Meditation and Life
by Swami Chinmayananda

Self-Unfoldment
by Swami Chinmayananda

THE *Hindu Culture* SERIES

Hindu Culture: An Introduction
by Swami Tejomayananda

For information contact:
Chinmaya Mission West Publications Division
Distribution Office
560 Bridgetown Pike
Langhorne, PA 19053, USA
Phone: (215) 396-0390 Fax: (215) 396-9710
Toll Free: 1-888-CMW-READ (1-888-269-7323)

The Sanskrit word *Mananam* means reflection. The *Mananam* series of books is dedicated to the exposition of Vedantic thought, with an emphasis on the unity of all religions. It is published by Chinmaya Mission West, which was founded by Swami Chinmayananda in 1975. Swami Chinmayananda pursued the spiritual path in the Himalayas, under the guidance of Swami Sivananda and Swami Tapovanam. He is credited with the awakening of India and the rest of the world to the ageless wisdom of Vedanta. He taught the logic of spirituality and emphasized that selfless work, study, and meditation are the cornerstones of spiritual practice. His legacy remains in the form of books, audio and video tapes, schools, social service projects, and Vedanta teachers who now serve their local communities all around the world.